TRANSLATING STRATEGY INTO ACTION

DUKE CORPORATE EDUCATION

TRANSLATING STRATEGY INTO ACTION

Dearborn™
Trade Publishing
A **Kaplan Professional** Company

President, Dearborn Publishing: Roy Lipner
Vice President and Publisher: Cynthia A. Zigmund
Acquisitions Editor: Jonathan Malysiak
Senior Project Editor: Trey Thoelcke
Interior Design: Lucy Jenkins
Cover Design: Design Solutions
Typesetting: Elizabeth Pitts

Published by Dearborn Trade Publishing
A Kaplan Professional Company

Printed in the United States of America

05 06 07 10 9 8 7 6 5 4 3 2

Library of Congress Cataloging-in-Publication Data

Duke Corporate Education.
    Translating strategy into action / Duke Corporate Education.
        p.   cm. — (Leading from the center)
    Includes bibliographical references and index.
    ISBN 0-7931-9520-9
1. Strategic planning. 2. Industrial management. I. Title. II. Series.
    HD30.28.D838 2005
    658.4'012—dc22
                                                2005002820

CONTENTS

ACKNOWLEDGMENTS

First and foremost, we want to thank our clients and the many program participants around the globe. We begin our work by listening to our clients and gaining an understanding of their business challenges. Working with talented clients and actively engaging in their challenges across a range of industries and geographies has afforded us the opportunity to learn and develop an informed point of view on these topics. We thank our clients for trusting in our approach and making us part of their team.

We are also fortunate to have an extensive network of faculty, coaches, facilitators, and partners who believe in our mission and have opted to join in our adventure. Together, we have delivered programs in 37 different countries since we formed in July 2000. We absolutely could not have accomplished what we have and learned what we know without them.

John Tolsma and his colleagues at erroyo have been a close partner for several years. As John worked with us, he came to believe that we have something unique to say and urged us to capture our ideas in these books. He introduced us to our editors at Dearborn Trade and the rest, as they say, is history. Jon Malysiak and Trey Thoelcke have patiently guided us through this process. We can't thank them enough.

As with any organization, we too have created a shorthand that accelerates our own conversation, but doesn't translate well outside Duke CE. We were lucky to have the writing and editing assistance of a local writer, Elizabeth Brack. Betsy worked with us over the many versions and edits of these chapters to make the words flow more smoothly.

Throughout the book you will see several graphical images reinforcing the surrounding ideas. Ryan Stevens worked with us patiently to capture our thoughts and ideas into the graphical images included within the book, often working with vague instructions such as, "it should feel like 'this.'" He did a wonderful job.

We especially thank Judy Rosenblum, our chief operating officer, for her invaluable input. Given her strategy background and experience, her insight and guidance in helping us articulate the strategic concepts and the guiding ideas within the Breakthrough Model was essential to this endeavor.

Without a doubt the busiest person at Duke CE, our CEO Blair Sheppard, was instrumental to this effort. He supported the initiative from the outset and more importantly always made time to review our output, and guide our thinking. His assistance is without measure. We could not have done it without him.

During the many weeks we've spent working on this book—engaging clients, researching, talking, writing, editing, and then cycling back to the beginning—we came across a statement one day that essentially said no great works (musical compositions, novels, and the like) can be created by a team—the thought being that they require the guiding vision and creativity of a single, uniquely talented individual. Although our book certainly isn't in the category of great literary works, we take immense pride that this, like our client work, has been indeed very much a team effort.

We've drawn upon the insight, experience, and expertise from numerous colleagues here at Duke CE. We hope that the content of this book stimulates your thinking and improves your ability to act and solve the strategic challenges confronting you.

The *Translating Strategy into Action* book team: Michael Canning, Marla Tuchinsky, Cindy Campbell, and Kati Clement-Frazier.

INTRODUCTION

In the past 30 years, they have been repeatedly laid off, outsourced, replaced by information technology (IT) applications, and insulted with such derogatory names as "the cement layer." Their bosses accused them of distorting and disrupting communication in their organizations, and their subordinates accused them of thwarting the subordinates' autonomy and empowerment. Who are "they"? Middle managers, those managing in the middle of the organization.

With such treatment, you might think that middle managers are villainous evildoers who sabotage companies or obstructionist bureaucrats who stand in the way of real work getting done. However, the reality is just the opposite. When performed well, the middle manager role is critical in organizations.

Although over the past several decades the value and stature of middle managers has seen both high and low points, we at Duke Corporate Education believe that managing in the middle of the organization has always been both critically important and personally demanding. As one would expect, the essence of the role—the required mind-set and skill set—has continued to change over time. The need to update both of these dimensions is driven by periodic shifts in such underlying forces as marketplace dynamics, technology, organizational structure, and employee expectations. Now and then, these forces converge to create a point of inflection that calls for a "step change" in how organizations are governed, with particular implications for those managing in the center.

In the *Leading from the Center* series, we examine some of these primary causes that are shaping what it means to successfully lead from the center in the modern organization. We outline the emerging imperative for middle management in an organization as well as the mind-set, knowledge, and skills required to successfully navigate through the most prevalent challenges that lie ahead.

THE NEW CENTER

There are four powerful and pervasive trends affecting the role that managers in the center of an organization are being asked to assume. These trends—information technology, industry convergence, globalization, and regulations—connect directly to the challenges these managers are facing.

Compared to 20 or 30 years ago, *information technology* has escalated the amount, speed, and availability of data to the point that it has changed the way we work and live. Access to information has shifted more power to our customers and suppliers. They not only have more information, but are directly involved in and interacting with the various processes along the value chain. On a personal level, we now find ourselves connected to other people all the time—cell phones, pagers, BlackBerrys, and PDAs all reinforce the 24/7 culture. The transition from workweek to weekend and back is less distinct. These micro-transitions happen all day, every day because many of us remain connected all the time.

Industries previously seen as separate are now seeing multiple points of *convergence*. Think about how digital technology has led to a convergence of sound, image, text, computing, and communications. Longstanding industry boundaries and parameters are gone (e.g., cable television companies are in the phone business, electronics companies sell music), and along with them, the basis and nature of competition. The boundaries are blurred. It's clear that new possibilities, opportunities, and directions exist, but it isn't always clear what managers should do. Managers will have to be prepared to adapt; their role is to observe, learn from experience, and set direction dynamically. Layered on top of this is the need to manage a more complex set of relationships—cooperating on Monday, competing on Tuesday, and partnering on Wednesday.

Globalization means that assets are now distributed and configured around the world to serve customers and gain competitive advantage. Even companies that consider themselves local interact with global organizations. There is more reliance on fast-developing regional centers of expertise, for example, computer programming in India and manufacturing in China. This means that middle managers are interacting with and coordinating the efforts of people who live in different cultures, and may be awake while the managers are asleep. The notion of a workday has changed as the work straddles time zones. The nature of leading has changed as it becomes more common to partner with vendors and work in virtual teams across regions.

The first three forces are causing shifts in the fourth—the *regulatory environment.*

Many industries are experiencing more regulation, while a few others are experiencing less. In some arenas now experiencing more regulation, there is also a drive for more accountability. Demand for more accountability leads to a greater desire to clarify boundaries and roles. Yet there is more ambiguity as to what the rules are and how best to operationalize them. Consider how, in the wake of Sarbanes-Oxley legislation, U.S. companies and their accountants continue to sort through the new requirements, while rail companies in Britain are negotiating which company is responsible for maintaining what stretch of tracks. Middle managers sit where regulations get implemented and are a critical force in shaping how companies respond to the shifts in the environment.

All of these changes have implications for those managing at the center of organizations. No small group at the top can have the entire picture because the environment has more of everything: more information and connectivity, a faster pace, a dynamic competitive space, greater geographic reach, better informed and connected customers and suppliers, and shifting legal rules of the game. No small group can process the implications, make thoughtful decisions and disseminate clear action steps. The top of the organization needs those in the center to help make sense of the dynamic environment. The connection between strategy development and strategy execution becomes less linear and more interdependent and, therefore, managers in the center become pivotal actors.

As we said earlier, the notion of the middle of an organization typically conjures up a vertical image depicting managers in the center of a hierarchy. This mental image carries with it a perception of those managers as gatekeepers—controlling the pace at which information or resources flow down or up. It appears to be simple and linear.

However, as many of you are no doubt experiencing, you now find yourselves navigating in a matrix, and as a node in a network or

FIGURE I.1 In the Center of the Action

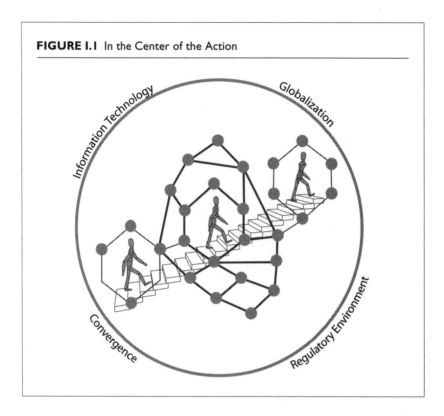

multiple networks. As depicted in Figure I.1, this new view of the center conjures up images of centrality, integration, connection, and catalyst. *You are in the center of the action, not the middle of a hierarchy.* When you overlay this connected view on the traditional vertical notion, it produces some interesting tensions, trade offs, and opportunities. Your formal authority runs vertically, but your real power to achieve results stems from your ability to work across all levels and boundaries.

IF YOU ARE LEADING FROM THE CENTER

If you are a manager in the center today, you have many hats to wear, more balls to juggle, and fewer certainties in your work environment. You have to be adaptive yet provide continuity in your leadership. You need to simultaneously translate strategy, influence and collaborate, lead teams, coach and motivate your people, support innovation, and own the systems and processes—all in the service of getting results. Those in the center need more courage than ever. You are the conscience of your organizations, carrying forth the values, at the same time you build today and tomorrow's business success.

Strategy Translator

As a strategy translator, you must first understand the corporate strategy and determine what parts of it your group can best support. Next, you must translate it into an action plan for your group, making sure it aligns well to the overall strategy. You'll need to consider which projects are essential stepping stones and which are needed in their own right, and establish some priorities or guiding goals. You must then communicate the details of the plan and priorities, and create momentum around them. As your team implements, you'll need to involve not only your people but to also collaborate and coordinate with others, including peers, customers, and other units. Instead of directing a one-way downward flow of information, you must translate upward as well and act as a conduit for strategic feedback to the executives above.

Influencer and Collaborator for Results

Middle managers must learn how to make things happen by influencing, integrating, and collaborating across the boundaries of the organization. As a manager, instead of focusing exclusively on your piece, you have to look outside of your own group to develop a network of supporting relationships. Rather than issuing commands and asserting power based on your position, you have to use other tactics to gain agreement and make things happen.

Leader of Teams

Teams have become a one-size-fits-all solution for organizing work in today's economy—virtual teams, project teams, product teams, and function-specific teams—and can be either the blessing or the bane of many companies. Your role as a manager includes understanding the challenges of teams and facilitating their development so that they can be effective more quickly. You have to align the team's energy and talents in a way that will deliver the desired results. You are responsible for creating an environment that will help this group of people work well together to achieve today's objectives and to develop the skills needed to take on future goals.

Coach and Motivator

While many organizations are well positioned to execute their strategies in yesterday's environment, they are moderately able to meet their current needs and often they are not thinking about how to position themselves for the future. From the center of the organization, middle managers assume much of the responsibility for their people. They create an environment to attract and retain good employees, coach them to do their current jobs better, and bear primary responsibility for developing others. As a manager, you must figure out how to build the next level of capability, protect existing people, connect their aspirations to opportunities for development, and make work more enjoyable. You need to provide regular feedback—both positive and redirecting—and build strong relationships with those who surround you. If done well, your departments will be more efficient and your employees will be better equipped to become leaders in their own right.

Intrapreneur/Innovator

Enabling and supporting an innovative approach within your company will foster the strategic direction of the future. To effectively sponsor innovation, you need to create the context for your people, foster a climate that supports innovative efforts, and actively sponsor the ideas of the future. You have to *be* innovative and *lead* the innovative efforts of others. Innovation is most often associated with new-product development, but innovative approaches also are needed in developing new services or solving internal system and process problems. As a manager, you use their influence and relationships to find the root cause of problems, and the resources to make change happen.

Owner of Systems and Processes

Managers need to understand that part of their role is to take ownership for architecting new systems and processes. You have to shift your thinking from living within existing systems and processes to making sure that those systems and processes work well: Do the systems and processes support or get in the way of progress? One of the mistakes we have made in the past is to not hold managers accountable for their role in architecting the next generation of systems and processes. As a manager, you must perform harsh audits of existing systems, and understand when to tear down what may have been left in place from a past strategy. You need to assess what is no longer relevant and/or is no longer working. Part of your responsibility is to think about and decide whether to reengineer or remove existing systems.

SHIFT IN MIND-SET NEEDED FOR THE FUTURE

Overcoming the challenges and seizing the opportunities of Leading from the Center requires a shift in mindset and skill set. To be successful in this more dynamic and interconnected world, you need to understand your company's strategy; translate that strategy in a way that creates meaning and increases the alignment and commitment of your team; and define the key priorities and activities that your team will pursue. It's a challenging but critical task. Over the next seven chapters we will outline a process and offer a set of tools and techniques that will enable you to effectively translate strategy into action and results.

CHAPTER ONE

THE CHALLENGE OF TRANSLATING STRATEGY

IN THIS CHAPTER

Strategy: Harder to Create, Harder to Execute ■ New
World Requires New Approaches to Strategy ■ Implications
for Strategy Development and Execution ■ Manager as
Translator ■ What's to Follow in This Book

If you were asked what changes in the environment have had the
most profound impact on how we think about business strategy, what
would you answer? Would you reply, "The Internet and information
technology"? Or do you think globalization has changed business
strategy the most?

The confluence of several trends have forever altered the marketplace and are causing a fundamental shift in how companies think
about and execute strategy. These trends, depicted in Figure 1.1,
have caused the manager's role in developing and executing strategy
to become both more important *and* more complex. Information
technology continues to improve and advance at a rapid pace. Increased globalization has led to more intense and different types of
competition. Shifts in the regulatory environment have opened up
new avenues for some companies. In addition, the growing merger
of companies across industries has changed the business environment dramatically.

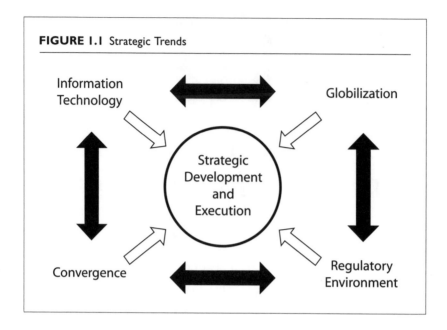

FIGURE 1.1 Strategic Trends

Add to all of this the implications of a demographically chang-ing workforce. Life expectancy has risen, and an aging workforce is a worldwide phenomenon. While mature workers are extending their time before retirement, there are also fewer people entering the workforce, and growing concern that there will not be enough new workers to replace the retiring Baby Boomers. All of which has strategic management implications for workforce capability plan-ning: how to attract and retain experienced workers, how to plan for transfer of their critical knowledge and skills, and how to make the workplace flexible and accessible for older workers. In addition, we now see three to four generations present in the workforce, with dif-ferent expectations about what "work" means and how it fits in their lives, making the manager's task even more complex.

STRATEGY
Harder to Create, Harder to Execute

The intent of business strategy remains largely the same: It fo-cuses on the question, *How can we shape the future to our advantage and create and capture a greater share of economic value?* However, the trends noted above force managers to question some long-held and important beliefs and practices associated with strategy development and execution.

As managers, the combination of more information, a faster pace, greater geographic reach, greater interdependence, and elevated scrutiny means the environment we manage and the problems we face are increasingly complex—there are more people, more time zones, more options, *and* less time to respond.

Many managers we've worked with at Duke Corporate Education have expressed this as the "AND" challenge: Solutions need to be more systemic *and* implemented faster, sustainable *and* flexible, high quality *and* delivered using fewer resources, customized *and* scaleable. Managing these apparent paradoxes is no longer the exception, but the norm.

In a practical sense, managers in the center have always been the glue that holds the organization together, aligns the organization, and makes things happen. They are the ones who take the overall company strategy and make sense out of it, and they ensure that it is translated into action and results. As translators, they make abstract concepts real and actionable, and act as sense makers, helping their direct reports and team members to understand not only what to do but why. What happens when these managers in the center don't understand the strategy themselves and fail to create meaning or make connections for their people? What happens when they or their teams either don't believe the strategy, or see the "new strategy" as yet another change that may or may not be "real"? They may hope it goes away like the others if they just stay as they are and ignore it. Then they essentially *do* become a blockage in the middle—slowing things down, failing to make the right choices—leading to entropy, not action and results.

Understanding the underlying trends driving these fundamental shifts helps managers realize that the changes they're experiencing are not in fact going to blow over, but rather are irreversible and accelerating. Today, these new marketplace challenges have raised the bar and made the work of translating strategy into action and results more challenging. To do this effectively, managers must reorient themselves, expand their knowledge, and adopt and practice new methods and tools.

NEW WORLD REQUIRES NEW APPROACHES TO STRATEGY

The trends noted in Figure 1.1 are affecting strategy creation in many ways. The quick adoption and widespread use of Internet technologies has allowed easier and broader access to information: businesses provide details of their products or services on the Web; customers share experiences and opinions with one another; and shopping for price and features is relatively easy. In short, widespread use of the Internet has resulted in better informed, more knowledgeable customers with greater leverage.

Think about eBay's structure. Customers have the opportunity to rate sellers on the accuracy of their product descriptions, their helpfulness during the selling process, and the speed with which they mail items. This involvement has a direct effect on how well a seller succeeds. This trend has irreversibly changed customer expectations, shifted the balance of power, and changed purchasing patterns and behaviors.

The technology revolution has made it easy for people to get all sorts of information—on their customers, their competition, and changes in the environment. Easy access has leveled the playing field, allowing fewer "trade secrets" to persist. Most firms now have access to the same customer, market, and strategic data as their competitors do. Everyone is learning more about the marketplace and doing it with ease, so the "shelf life" of information continues to decrease. When taken together, it implies that implementing a strategy successfully requires managers to move from data acquisition to insight. *How managers make sense of information is what will set them and their companies apart.*

On the other hand, easy access to data has increased the amount of information managers need to evaluate. It is difficult for one person alone to piece together a coherent picture. People will need to work together to filter and interpret information. Competitive edge today will come more from the *insight* that managers are able to draw from the data rather than from the data itself.

Add to this trend the fact that the pace and depth of globalization are intensifying. In the past, for U.S.–based firms, globalization meant extending the geographic reach of products and services. Now we see the impact of two trends. First, the breaking apart of the value chain. Companies have significant portions of their value chain—such as key suppliers, vendors and partners—distributed around the world in an effort to better serve customers and gain a competitive edge from the emerging regional centers of expertise.

Second, the growing economic power of a few significant emerging markets, namely China, India, Brazil, and Russia, is now changing the global playing field. Their large and fast-growing populations, with different distributions of wealth and comparative advantages, pose radical challenges to more traditional organizations. Those in an established market must figure out how to compete with and serve these growing economic tigers.

Simultaneous deregulation in many geographies and markets and reregulation in others have disrupted the business status quo. Regulations governed the space, geographies, and industry in which firms could play as well as the rules of engagement. As these legal frameworks are adapted and loosened to meet the new sociopolitical realities and challenges, competition increases in unusual patterns. Conversely, in many industries, not just financial services, increased regulation and scrutiny are forcing companies to redefine themselves and their practices with limited concrete guidance. This upheaval of certain long-standing conditions or "givens" creates both new risk and opportunity. The rules of engagement are evolving and being defined dynamically through actual practice and experience. Navigating in this ambiguous, ever-changing world requires that managers actively engage and experiment with new approaches, "go to market" strategies, and organizational forms as they work to understand and harness the dynamism in the marketplace.

In recent years, many long-standing industry definitions and structures have been rapidly collapsing and converging. One of the most dramatic examples has been driven by the discovery and commercialization of digital technology. This technology has rocked the long-standing strategic foundation and irrevocably blurred industry boundaries between music, entertainment, publishing, consumer electronics, and telecommunication companies. As these boundaries and assumptions regarding strategy and competition are challenged, companies find themselves simultaneously competing in unfamiliar terrain, responding to new challenges, and collectively creating new industry logic. This marketplace vitality demands a faster pace and greater level of integration between the strategy development and execution processes. In this environment, taking action; understanding what worked, what didn't, and why; and providing insightful feedback become a critical part of the strategy development process.

IMPLICATIONS FOR STRATEGY DEVELOPMENT AND EXECUTION

Many companies find themselves competing in a new and different game. Another example of an industry undergoing change is the newspaper industry. An industry once in the business of simply printing news, it now has to redefine its product as information; it can no longer define itself by the medium in which the news is delivered. Those within this industry face several strategic concerns: How should they be migrating to the Internet? Are they making any money with their online venture? Does their Web news cannibalize their traditional product or increase readership? How do they define their competition? To complicate matters, the Web has niche or specialized publishers who have already mastered the technology. As these new strategies are woven through the organizations, local paper editors and section editors have to make decisions about what goes in print, what goes on the Web, and how to position themselves in these two marketplaces.

Traditional supermarkets are competing with Wal-Mart, Costco, and Super Target on the one side and specialty stores, such as Whole Foods, EarthFare, Trader Joe's, and specialty ethnic food shops, on the other. The telephone industry is crossing into television. Banks are getting involved in insurance. The Sarbanes-Oxley Act is altering the landscape for accounting firms, forcing changes to their business models. These are but a few examples of how the new trends are affecting business.

Changes in technology can even drive out a traditional business, forcing a company to reposition itself by entering new markets. Consider the Columbus Washboard Company. Founded in 1895, it hit peak sales and production during World War II. With the advent of washing machines, market demand declined. By the 1970s, Colum-

Let's use an example to illustrate. Since the invention of basketball in 1891 by Dr. James Naismith, the game has essentially remained the same. Certain technical changes have occurred over time to help the game adapt to new conditions, such as the size of the ball, the height of the rim, and the three-point line. The fundamental assumptions surrounding the game, however, have remained largely intact. Therefore, the context and assumptions on which a good strategy is built are known—hire the best coach, recruit the best players for each role, play to your team's strengths (e.g., passing game versus running game versus iron-clad defense), practice and more practice, scout the competition, and outplay the other team. The challenges involved in positioning your team for success in a competitive league are substantial, but known. And, of course, in the end, it also comes down to execution.

In contrast, occasionally a more disruptive change occurs where both the technical rules and the underlying logic of the competitive landscape shift simultaneously, as happened with ice hockey. Ice hockey can trace its origins to field hockey. Northern Europeans liked the summer game so much that they adapted it to winter conditions. Although there were many similarities originally, a new game with different technical rules and different underlying logic emerged. It's fair to say that a field hockey team today would not fare very well on the other playing field. It requires different strategies and capabilities.

Early entrants to this new sport with different technical rules and underlying logic faced multiple challenges. First, they had to carefully discern what portions of their previous experience, beliefs, and ideas could be adapted for this new game; field positions could stay but running could not. Second, the coach may have set a strategic direction but the players and the coach had to embrace active experimentation, learn quickly, and adapt the strategy based on their actual experience. Ice hockey was originally played with nine players. When a team turned up short-handed, their opponent agreed to have two players sit out. Players decided they liked the smaller team better, and the change became permanent. The earlier teams had a distinct advantage—they got to influence the rules and conditions of play. (Davidson, 1997) bus was the only washboard manufacturer left in the United States. It had gained market share as each of its competitors exited, but the overall market was dwindling. In 1987, the company decided to take a new approach. They still would cater to customers who used a washboard for laundry, such as soldiers in the field and the Amish, but they would expand into specialty washboards for musicians and crafts and furniture that used washboards.

Access to information and increased competition will continue to force companies to develop strategy at the same time as they execute it. Companies will have to place big bets without complete information, forcing changes in the strategy and requiring capabilities to be built during the execution process. Consider the saying "changing a tire while the car is moving," and you get the idea. The strategy development process now requires real-time learning and feedback as execution occurs. The two processes become more of an interactive system than a linear process. This further implies that strategy development can no longer remain the territory of a very small team at the top of the organization. This more dynamic strategy system demands an increase in both the number of people involved and the level of their collaboration.

MANAGER AS TRANSLATOR

As the marketplace becomes more dynamic and the pace of change accelerates over the next decade, the work for those in the center of the organization will become even more lively and essential. Because the information about the future will be incomplete and time is of the essence, companies are forced to place bets on a strategic direction and work out the details at the same time they are implementing the strategy. Because the strategy is being executed in real time through the action of multiple actors, the amount of information about the future will often seem incomplete and the planning horizon short. Companies are therefore forced to iterate and adjust the details of how to achieve their strategy. By way of analogy, imagine hiking to a mountaintop. Your destination is pretty much fixed; the mountaintop isn't going to move and, for the most part, you can keep it in sight. You have a general route mapped out, but can't yet see what lies ahead. You will encounter obstacles along the

FIGURE 1.2 Manager's Roles

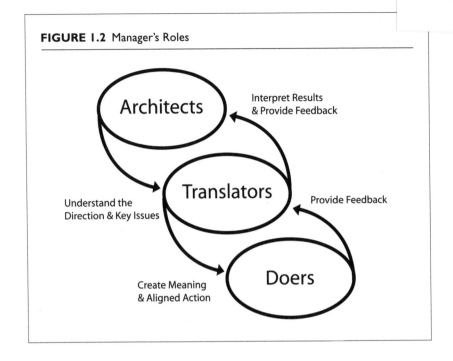

way—some anticipated and some not. You'll have to adapt and adjust as you go, determining the best way to continue making progress around rocks, ground water, and downed trees. Sometimes, you cut a new path.

As Figure 1.2 demonstrates, leaders in the center of the organization have always played a pivotal role in effectively translating strategy into action and results. Today, as in the past, they must understand the strategy and understand how their group directly connects to it and supports it. Next, they need to make these connections clear to their team in a way that creates meaningful connections and priorities. Managers must plan work, figuring out how to stage and sequence their team's actions for maximum leverage. Finally, they need to develop capabilities to enable execution today and build the foundation for a tomorrow that has yet to be defined. The complexity of today's environment and the pace at which the future is being created dictate that today's manager has to think about strategic direction and its implications for daily work on a continual basis. Strategy is no longer a plan that is worked on once a year or even occasionally. The market is more dynamic and therefore so must be the strategy translation process. Managers in the center today have to be active. You can't achieve the necessary results simply by reacting to the dynamics, and you can't sustain the effort that it takes to be in a constant mode of response. Be proactive. Study and learn more about both your business and the world around it.

Managers can't anticipate and solve every issue. They need to connect with and actively engage their people, not only in executing a plan to implement solutions, but also in playing an active role in developing those solutions. Workers need to be adept in adjusting to shifting strategies, interpreting data, and collaborating for results in order to execute well.

Duke Corporate Education teams interact with many potential clients who come to us thinking that they have a strategy problem: "Somehow the strategy isn't working." In many cases, though, these executives really are facing an execution problem. Their strategy may be appropriate on paper, but they run into trouble bringing it to life.

WHAT'S TO FOLLOW IN THIS BOOK

This book outlines a process and contains practical tools and techniques that will help you translate and execute strategy into action and results. In addition to these tools and techniques, your success in this endeavor also depends largely on your ability to enact the following five principles:

1. *Be a student.* Study your business and the broader world. Study your environment, your competitors, and how you make money, then look at how other industries and institutions are changing to see any similarities. Read broadly, because in a dynamic world, the change within your business is going to come from an unexpected place.
2. *Create meaning.* Given the uncertainties and continuous change in your own business, your direct reports and those who work for them are increasingly unsure. Your job is not just to translate strategy into goals and action steps (the easy part). You also must help them understand the larger context for the strategy. Outline the reasons for the uncertainty and apparent

ambiguity, provide real assurance that it can work, build understanding, and connect the strategy to things they care about and are working on. Being a student of the business furthers your own understanding and will, in turn, help you create meaning for others through better explanations, analogies in other industries, and evidence that something like this has worked in other places. Think of the strategy as a story, and learn how to tell one.

3. *Be honest.* Strategy translation and execution always entails moving from where you are to where you want to be. Without an honest and incisive analysis of where you are, this journey begins on faulty ground. Particularly difficult is that this assessment is predicated on the direction implied by the strategy—assessing current reality is never context free, and in today's world, future vision is never as clear as we would like. Thus, it is doubly important that we be truly honest about our present performance, our assets, the strength of our partner relations, the limitations of our processes and systems, and, most importantly, the capability of our people and ourselves.

4. *Think capabilities.* Most people think that having translated goals into sequenced action steps, targets, and goals, and the work to be done, their translation job is over and it is now time to move to execution. The more important step is to focus on building the capabilities necessary to achieve these steps and ultimately the intended vision. First, all change in strategy entails some change in capabilities, and without a focus on these capabilities the strategy will fail. Second, by working on developing new capabilities, the strategy comes to life for everyone, develops personal meaning and adds value to the individual. Third, the action steps will change, but the capabilities provide an asset for the next vision. Capabilities sustain longer in a dynamic world and are the real basis of competitive advantage. Included in these capabilities are the set of relations you have within the firm and outside the firm. (See *Influencing and Collaborating for Results,* another book in the Leading from the Center series.)

5. *Get comfortable with change.* Continue to learn how to adapt because the degree and pace of change is increasing. As outlined

in this chapter, we live in an increasingly dynamic world, thus, your firm's strategy *will* change, maybe not in major ways, but always in subtle and important ways. Embrace this change as the reason you have a job, and be proactive. Develop the skills necessary to lead in a continuously changing world and build a depth of understanding of the strategic context in yourself and your employees. Give them meaning so that they can manage the paradox of executing with passion the strategy as it presently exists, while acknowledging its half-life is getting increasingly short. You only get to play in the next round if you win in this one, but winning in this one puts you at risk as the rules change. Welcome to the 21st Century.

The chapters that follow lay out the process, key concepts, tools, and approaches that will help you to translate strategy into action. By the end of Chapter 7, you will have numerous tips on how to approach this role as we cover the following areas:

- Understanding the strategic direction and key issues
- Translating strategy into a meaningful plan that drives the day-to-day work and results
- Aligning short-term decisions and actions with a bigger picture and long-term goals
- Understanding and dealing with operational interdependencies
- Engaging people's hearts and brains in the execution of the strategy

CHAPTER TWO

STRATEGY 101

IN THIS CHAPTER

Why We Need to Understand Strategy ■ Elements of a Good
Strategy ■ Regional Interpretations of Strategy ■ Change
Is a Given ■ Understanding Your Strategy

WHY WE NEED TO UNDERSTAND STRATEGY

What is strategy? What are the elements of a good strategy? How
do you know if you have a good strategy? Do you understand your
company's strategy well enough to create meaning out of it for your
group? Can you make the alignment connections between the corporate strategy, the divisional strategy, and your group's action plan?
Are you using this strategy as a basis for your goals and objectives?
Does it guide the decisions that you make on a daily basis and help
you prioritize multiple demands?

Before we answer any of the above questions, let's begin with
making sense of strategy in general. When asked to define their corporate strategy, many people fall back on their corporate mission,
what their business is, what their products are, superlatives ("We
strive to be the best in our industry"), or even define themselves by

their customers or geographic region. These can all be *elements* of a strategy, but alone are not "the strategy."

The word *strategy* has become a generalized word that means different things to different people and different companies. The word's meaning has been diluted with overuse. As noted by Hambrick and Fredrickson (2001), when we call everything a strategy, the organization can end up with a collection of strategic messages that create confusion and misalignment.

Strategy is about being different and making choices. The intent of a business strategy is to define how the company can shape the future to its advantage and create and capture a greater share of the economic value. It outlines where and how the company will compete and gives some structure to what you are trying to accomplish. It also provides direction, guidance, and focus when you are faced with choices. If people in the organization don't understand how the company is supposed to be different and what opportunities they are to pursue, how can they make the touch choices that they have to make every day? (Porter, 1980) Without a strategy, a company and its managers can flounder without direction, wasting time, energy, and resources.

As depicted in Figure 2.1, it's a dynamic process, adapting and changing over time. As managers across an organization provide feedback, the company's strategy may be adjusted to incorporate this new information about shifting geographic trends, customer needs, regulations, competitors, technologies, or partners. Changes to any of the elements that compose the strategy may create the need for adjustment. As the corporate strategy shifts, so may the various divisions. Depending on which areas of the strategy you support, your team may need to adjust its focus as well.

Creating strategic context for your team creates a greater sense of purpose by connecting what they are doing to the bigger picture. It also helps them either to understand the reason for shifts when they do occur or to anticipate and suggest shifts themselves. Can you currently describe the goals and objectives of your team in a way that allows team members to connect what they're working on to the bigger picture?

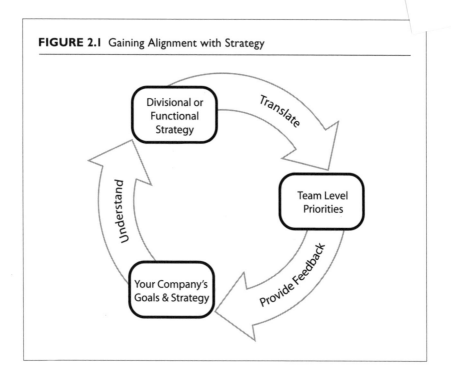

FIGURE 2.1 Gaining Alignment with Strategy

ELEMENTS OF A GOOD STRATEGY

What may be clearer than a strict definition of strategy is to consider various strategic models used by organizations to help articulate their strategy. On the surface, each model may have a different number of factors, use alternative language or guiding questions, and sort information into different categories.

How the information is organized and labeled is less important than whether the core strategic questions are addressed and whether people fully understand the implications of the answers. Remember, strategy will always be in a state of flux and should be adaptable to today's fast-paced environment. The "players" in the game are constantly on the move and you have to be ready to adapt to the game. Regardless of the model used, building your understanding of the strategy requires that you have a working knowledge of environment, strategic direction, business model, and organizational capabilities. (See Figure 2.2.)

Hambrick and Fredrickson Strategic Model

Donald Hambrick and James Fredrickson (2001) developed the strategy diamond, featuring five key questions to consider:

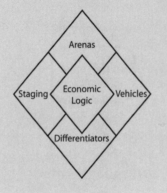

Arenas: Where will we be active?

Vehicles: How will we get there?

Differentiators: How will we win (versus our competition) in the marketplace?

Staging: What will be our speed and sequence of moves?

Economic Logic: How will we make money?

Environment

Environment is the larger context in which the company operates and your strategy is situated. The industry in which you operate will have a strong impact on your strategy.

Understanding your environment and the key trends and forces shaping it is essential to understanding your opportunities and how to craft a strategy to seize them. This relates to the fundamental forces outlined in Chapter 1. In order to be successful in your role, you need to be well-grounded in the essential environmental factors driving your strategic choices and broaden your understanding of how the conduct of strategy has changed given the complex and dynamic nature of the environment.

Managers will continue to be confronted with trade offs and be expected to make decisions quickly, even while the strategy itself continues to evolve. Therefore, having more than a cursory understanding of the *why* underlying the strategy is essential to informing and expanding the mangers' perspective and judgment.

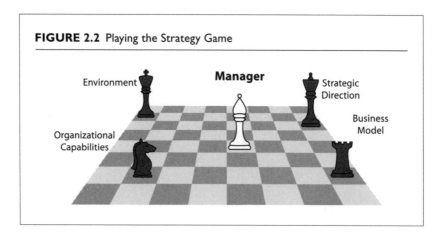

FIGURE 2.2 Playing the Strategy Game

Answer the following questions in terms of your own company's *environment:*

- What are the major trends shaping your industry?
  - Customer demographics?
  - Investment patterns?
  - Regulatory environment or government policy changes?
- How do key constituents (e.g., shareholders, customers, analysts) view the trends?
- Who are your competitors? What are they doing now?
- What opportunities does this set of conditions create?

Strategic Direction

Strategic direction is what helps define the opportunities the company is going to pursue and how they intend to do so. It can comprise what markets you will serve, customers, geographies, lines of business, important brands and reputation. Strategic direction may also outline directly or by implication what opportunities you will *not* pursue and what markets the company will not play in.

Let's look at one major petroleum company and how they define their corporate strategy.

Long term, the Group aims to be world leader in energy and petrochemicals. Our goal is to deliver superior shareholder returns with a minimum commitment of sustaining dividends in real terms. Robust, sustained profitability and growth through competitive edge are key to this goal.

This strategic direction covers the corporate mission and company goals. The company further outlines their new strategy, which spells out the markets they serve, who the customers are, new geographical areas of operation, what lines of business the company will pursue, and its brand and reputation.

Developing Fuel for the Future

Demand for transport fuels will continue to grow across the world. Traditional gasoline and diesel fuels will play a major role in meeting that demand in the short to medium term. The Group continues to innovate to improve the performance of these conventional fuels and to reduce their impact on the environment.

We are also working on a range of projects to develop a new generation of fuels that will help to meet the challenges of providing sustainable transport. One of the most exciting developments in this area is our planned multi-billion dollar investment to build a Gas to Liquids (GTL) plant in _____. The GTL plant will provide ultra-clean fuels that offer significant environmental advantages, especially in urban areas with high air pollution.

GTL fuels will be a valuable addition to an increasingly competitive and sophisticated fuels market and are one example of our commitment to technological development and customer-focused innovation. They provide further diversity in our portfolio, giving the flexibility of converting natural gas into liquid products and building on the strong position we have established in LNG (liquid natural gas). Looking further ahead, we continue to support the development of alternative fuels derived from renewable sources and hydrogen. (Royal Dutch Petroleum, 2003)

From a corporate standpoint, the company's strategy is clearly defined; it's up to the company's managers to translate this strategic direction and align their groups to succeed. The company has noted its mission, its goals, how its goals will be measured, and the areas in which the company is doing and will be doing business, etc.

Let's look at the strategy behind one food company's products, the "meal enhancers" produced by H.J. Heinz. Meal enhancers—the ketchups, sauces, and condiments—are big business for the company. Heinz is facing increasing competition from three types of competitors: specialty products makers, such as "boutique" sauces; "me too" companies, such as store-brand ketchups; and traditional rivals, such as Hunt's. More and different competitors have increased the pressure on Heinz to maintain its number-one position. The company has had to develop a strategy to address these factors.

To maintain its global position as the leader in product sales of meal enhancers, the company developed its Brand Growth Strategy based on four imperatives: 1) drive profitable growth; 2) remove the clutter; 3) squeeze out costs; and 4) measure and recognize performance. Taking this strategy to heart, managers made changes within their groups. For example, some groups in the company developed new product lines to drive growth: "Upside-Down Ketchup," wildly-colored, kid-friendly ketchups, and specialty grilling sauces, to name a few. Some groups streamlined operations to "cut the clutter and squeeze out costs." With a clear strategic direction, managers were able to take steps to align their business and meet the company's new needs. (H.J. Heinz, 2003)

A pharmaceutical company based in India, Ranbaxy Laboratories defines its strategic direction by focusing on manufacturing and marketing generic pharmaceutical drugs. As one of the top ten generic drug companies in the world, Ranbaxy has developed its skill in managing exports, alliances, partnerships, and acquisitions to achieve profitability. Its growth strategy in India includes developing herbal brands for over-the-counter sales, expanding R&D to further enhance its generics business, and crafting new drugs and new drug delivery systems for future growth. (Ranbaxy, 2003)

Answer the following questions in terms of your own company's *strategic direction:*

- What is the nature of the opportunity?
- What do you want to be known for?
- What markets, geographies, products, and lines of business should you be active in?

- Who are the customers you want?
- What does your company brand stand for?
- How do you want to be positioned in the market?
- What are your overall goals?
- What are the key organizational initiatives that will help you achieve the strategy?

Business Model

This piece of the strategy can be thought of as how you will operationalize the strategic direction and the economic logic of how you will create and capture value as you pursue market opportunities. It includes considerations like your value proposition to your customers, channels served, product pricing, and revenue mix.

In the highly competitive banking industry, we can consider how the business model reflects the overall company strategy. BB&T Corporation, a financial holding company, has defined its strategy by the nature of its corporate holdings. Acquisition of community banks drives the business, with each community bank retaining its own regional president and, to some extent, its regional character. By doing this, the company allows local decisions to be made by the local bank's president; a distant, faceless bureaucrat has no part in day-to-day bank affairs, which makes the parent company fade into the background. BB&T touts its customer service as "more responsive, reliable, and empathetic," factors that distinguish it from other major national banks. Managers at BB&T, knowing the business model on which the company is based, can take action within the framework of the company's emphasis on community banking. (BB&T, 2004)

Answer the following questions in terms of your own company's *business model:*

- How will you operationalize your plans and make money?
- What is your value proposition to your clients?
- What customers and channel strategies will you pursue?
- What products or services do you need to offer, given the customers that you want?
- What revenue mix do you want?

- What alliances and partnerships will you need to execute your strategy?
- How will you measure success?
  - Economic factors?
  - Customer satisfaction ratings?
  - Market share?
  - Industry rankings?

Organizational Capabilities

When it comes to organizational capabilities, the first question is, What do we need to be capable of in order to execute the strategy and achieve our goals? The answer to this question varies widely across companies, based on their industry and strategy. You can think about these as the operational means necessary to enable the business model and execute the strategy. Once the required organizational capability has been identified, it then gets defined in terms of the unique combinations of work processes, systems, structure, people, work environment, and knowledge that comprise it.

Some companies build their business through a strong reputation and stable product line. They find a niche that matches well to their core skills and remain there. Over time, however, the environment changes, and that stable product line may no longer meet customers' needs. At that point, the company needs to reinvent itself, adjust, or close.

Kodak currently is involved in reinventing itself, bringing new products to market in an effort to compete in digital imaging. Growth in the photo-imaging business is not in film and developing but rather is in digital imaging and "must-have" new products, such as photo-quality printing paper, innovative cameras, and printers. Over the years, Kodak has spent more than $4 billion on research and development and has produced more than 4,000 U.S. patents, yet it doesn't have a significant number of "must-have" products in stores. To stay alive and relevant in its industry, Kodak needs to build organizational capability in digital imaging. This will require them to also develop a unique combination of cutting-edge knowledge of digital imaging, new work processes, and people with new skills and talents.

At least one group of scientists have broken out of the lab, and they have begun to sit with customers while they are using Kodak's medical imaging equipment. The scientists can see firsthand how customers use their products and what needs they can meet in their future products. These scientists have built new relationships with customers, changed their own product development processes, and shifted their perspective to include customers more strongly than before. By aligning more closely with customers, Kodak hopes to turn their patents into must-have products. (Rand, 2004)

Answer the following questions in terms of your own company's *organizational capabilities:*

- In what do you need to be world-class to achieve your strategy?
- What unique combination of capabilities—work processes, systems, structure, people, work environment, and knowledge—will you need to execute the strategy and achieve your goals?
- What must your organization look like and how must it operate to achieve your goals?

REGIONAL INTERPRETATIONS OF STRATEGY

Strategy is dynamic and not always well articulated or presented neatly and cleanly within the categories outlined. Depending on your particular organization, it may also undergo multiple translations as it filters through the various divisions, geographic regions, business units, and functional areas. In many cases, what reaches managers in the center are goals or targets accompanied by a slice of strategic messages. Information isn't being withheld, but the strategic context is often slim or full of gaps. As a leader your job is to find out more, fit the pieces of the puzzle together, and identify where your team or group fits within the broader strategy.

How and where will you get more information? Remember, be a student. Talk to people and learn from your network. Not just your boss, but others across the organization who may be able to fill in

Small Companies, Unique Challenges

Small companies, those with 200 or fewer employees, often don't have a well-articulated strategy. Many are start-up companies, run by dynamic and creative leaders who are more focused on rapid growth than on thinking through a business plan. These leaders may have left their previous jobs because of the rigid structure of "big business." Due to the focus on rapid growth, leaders are dealing with the immediate transitions and change instead of thinking ahead. Midlevel managers, especially those who may have come from larger companies, may find the lack of defined strategy difficult. The "flying by the seat of the pants" approach can become a problem, especially if the company's founders don't recognize when the time is right to formalize a business strategy, when to change hiring practices, and when to tighten up the operations. Growth will often force smaller companies to become more definitive with their strategy. Investors will want to see more formal plans that outline these elements, particularly their business plans.

Midlevel managers in small companies are likely to be more action-oriented and not as focused on the overall mission and goals of the company. Measurable goals and what areas the managers can influence may take precedence over focusing on the long-range plan. A lot of the company's particulars, such as its market, geographies, and lines of business, are more "verbal" than written. Managers learn by talking and interacting with employees, creating looser boundaries and less politics.

One line manager in a small manufacturing company wanted to improve her area's ability to prepare for future needs. She learned that one of the best ways to stay one step ahead of future needs was to build relationships with the divisions of the company that *were* more forward looking. By talking with the R&D and engineering sections, she could learn more about the new things that were under development and their anticipated time to production, thus giving her division some ability to prepare.

some of the gaps. Ferret out the strategic information contained in company documents such as:

- Analyst call reports
- Annual reports
- CEO presentations to stakeholders
- State of the Company addresses
- Big initiatives underway
- Customer surveys

CHANGE IS A GIVEN

The complexity and dynamics of the world in which we live makes answering strategy questions more difficult. Questions that used to be simple, such as "What industry are we in?," have become more complicated. Be prepared to adjust and realign with your strategy as it and the environment changes.

Take a look at the vodka market. Absolut, the most purchased vodka brand in the United States, is finding that its sales are being encroached on by new vodka brands entering the market. Consumers are gravitating to the new and different, with more and more vodka products threatening Absolut's position. Even though only a few of the new product launches will actually make it in the market, each one takes shelf space and attention away from Absolut's product.

In addition to stiffer and more abundant competition, Absolut was slow to move into the "super premium" vodka segment. This allowed others to get a strong foothold. The company launched its Level label in March 2004, long after the advent of Grey Goose and others in the $24-and-up price level. Once there, it performed well, contributing significantly to a 3.4 percent sales increase in 2004. To recover from the slow start, the company is in the midst of changing its marketing strategy; now turning toward marketing to specific target groups and customizing its advertising to appear to customers. (George and Jones, 2004)

Changes in the marketplace are shortening the lifecycle of corporate strategies. Strategies used to be delivered in three-year, five-year, or ten-year plans; now, the rapid pace of competition has accelerated the need to frequently reevaluate corporate strategy. Look again at the strategy questions in the previous section. Would your answers have been the same six months ago? A year ago?

UNDERSTANDING YOUR STRATEGY

Understanding your company's strategy as well as what causes volatility in your market are what enable you, the manager, to act quickly when adjustments need to be made, and to act without instructions.

Non Sequitur © 2004 Wiley Miller. Dist. by Universal Press Syndicate. Reprinted with permission. All rights reserved.

CHECKLIST

- ❏ Do you understand the basic elements of strategy?
- ❏ Do you understand your company's strategy within the elements described here?
- ❏ Which elements are clear? Which ones are not?
- ❏ Where can you go to learn more?
- ❏ Do you understand it well enough to make sense of it for others?

CHAPTER THREE

DEVELOPING A SHARED VISION

IN THIS CHAPTER

From Understanding to Action ■ Using Creative
Tension ■ Elements of a Vision ■ Developing Your
Vision of Results ■ Moving to a Shared Vision

So far, you have increased your understanding of your company's strategy and your regional or divisional strategy (if there is one). You also have considered which parts of the strategy your group does (or should) most directly support and influence. Your job now is to *translate that overall strategy into a coherent, compelling story and plan* that motivates and enables action for your group.

FROM UNDERSTANDING TO ACTION

One could argue that here is where the leaders in the center of the organization prove their value. They take high-level goals and direction, and create concrete action plans that their people can execute. They translate the strategy into real work in a way that inspires, informs, and directs.

So, how do you as a manager tackle this critical function? What's important and how do you go about it? First, you need to have a good handle on where the company is going in the next three years or so, including your company's overall direction; markets/geographies; what customers, products, and services you are targeting; and the like—all elements covered in Chapter 2. This is your starting point. From here you can situate your team within the overall organization and set up the team's vision and action plan. It's your job to create and ensure a good fit between the company's overall direction and your team-level vision. The better the fit, the more likely you will be to garner the resources required to get the work done and realize the economic value from the work done.

USING CREATIVE TENSION

At a foundational level, most people want to feel that they are informed and actively involved in creating a picture of the future, especially if they are expected to make it happen. They need to know the important elements of that picture, so they can actively engage in making it happen. They need to know that what they are working on makes a difference to the organization.

The Breakthrough Model shown in Figure 3.1 was developed by Judith Rosenblum, Duke Corporate Education's Chief Operating Officer. The approach has been used across a range of industries and has proven to be an effective tool for thinking about the process of translating strategy into action. The model is based on some fundamental beliefs about strategy.

- You must have a clear picture both of what you want (your vision) and what you have today (your current reality or situation). You need to also elaborate on *why* you are where you are today, otherwise, the gaps that you need to close are not clear.
- Capabilities are critical. Having the right capabilities to take advantage of key opportunities when they occur will give you a competitive advantage. Defining and developing the unique combination of capabilities needed to execute your strategy is an integral part of the plan.
- Strategies aim toward a destination and are staged in their execution. The staging and sequencing matters. (Wilhelm, 2003)

FIGURE 3.1 The Breakthrough Model

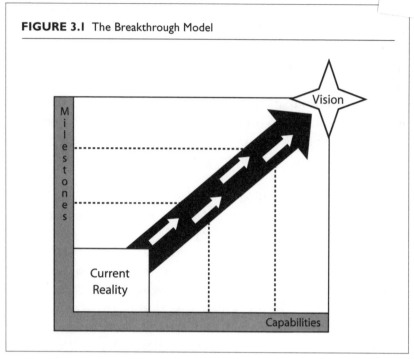

Source: © Judith Rosenblum

As a leader and translator of strategy, it's your job to engage your team in defining and making sense of these elements.

One basic principle underlying the Breakthrough Model is the notion of creative tension, sometimes also referred to as structural tension. Robert Fritz (1999) describes this tension as the pull between what you want (your vision) and the reality of what you have (your current situation). It's this tension that should *inform, inspire, and direct your actions.* It aligns and channels the energy of a team and generates the underlying force you need to mobilize people and achieve your goals.

"I can't say this strongly enough. This principle of structural tension—knowing what we want to create and knowing where we are in relationship to our goals—is the most powerful force an organization can have." (Robert Fritz, 1999)

Fritz notes that the word *tension* sometimes elicits connotations of stress or strain. However, creative tension is not intended to create emotional conflict or anxiety. Instead, it is a natural mechanism to generate and direct excitement, energy, and power. The more clarity, understanding, and relevant information you have regarding your vision *and* current situation, the greater your level of alignment; and the clearer a solution to bridge the differences will be. Bridging the difference essentially follows "the path of least resistance," because there is a natural inclination to move toward the desired state that works in your favor.

However, understanding creative tension as a manager requires more than strictly logical analysis. It is your job to engage people and create a shared vision. By focusing people's natural energy, you can create a sense of ownership and generate a deeper understanding among your team. The bottom line: *You get more leverage if you are aware of this tension and use it well than if you ignore it or fight it.*

Most of us have heard at least a portion of Dr. Martin Luther King, Jr.'s famous "I Have a Dream" speech, which he gave during the height of the civil rights movement. Rather than focusing only on the future, Dr. King began with describing the current conditions, creating a tension between the reality of today's situation and the vision of a better tomorrow. The message was clear: I know what it's like for you today, I'm not happy with the current situation and neither are you, and I want all of us to be in a better situation in the future. He ends his memorable speech with several "I have a dream" statements, reiterating the vision and inviting the audience to share his dream. Part of the power of the speech is its structure, from laying out the current situation through specific goals of achieving that vision (e.g., an end to segregated schools).

Consider one sales manager's situation. His department has a goal to establish a new market for their breakthrough product, the MegaThingamajig, and sell 50 units this year; however, the current reality is that only 5 have sold in the first quarter. The difference between the 5 products sold and the goal of selling 50 of them sets up the structural tension. The sales manager and his department have to develop a plan to reach their goal. Part of that plan would include a thorough assessment of where they are today.

Vision

- 50 MegaThingamajigs sold this year.
- Foundation laid to be market leader in the following year through good buzz and customer awareness.

Current Reality

- Which customers bought the 5 products we sold?
- Is there a major competitor? Where are they focusing their sales efforts?
- Does sales staff have enough training in the product?
- Is this a seasonal product, with higher sales expected in a later quarter?
- Have we introduced it in the right markets, with the right marketing campaign?
- Is it priced correctly?

In developing the plan, the manager might ask:

- Are there other, similar customers in our territory who might consider buying the product? Do we know them? If not, how can we get to know them?
- How can we expand our network to reach potential customers? Is there a group we need to join?
- What actions can we take to promote the product? Trade shows? Personal visits? Advertising?

Once the manager and sales team understand what the gap is and some potential ways to fill it, they should take two other steps as they craft a plan of action. First, they need to consider how to stage and sequence objectives and actions (particularly the critical first steps). Second, they should identify the required capabilities needed to execute what they have envisioned. We'll discuss these steps more in later chapters.

ELEMENTS OF A VISION

A vision is more than a statement, it's a snapshot of the future state you want to work toward. *The vision should elaborate what the group's members will be doing and how they will do it.* For example, what does your group need to look like for the role you've been assigned? What skills will your group need to have to serve internal or external customers? What environment do you need to create? One with stable routines or room to experiment? One that values questioning and reaches out to form relationships? One that encourages initiative? One that tightly controls quality? What processes or systems will you need to adopt, adapt, or create to support your work? You should incorporate answers to these questions into your vision.

What makes a good vision? Sir Winston Churchill, Mahatma Gandhi, even Abraham Lincoln—we are all familiar with their visionary speeches, filled with eloquently expressed ideas, goals, and dreams. They specified vividly what they saw as a problem, what a solution or resolution would look like, and the means to get there. They inspired people to share in their vision and help turn it into reality. Over the course of several speeches, these leaders highlighted themes and conjured images of what *could* be.

As a manager, you do the same, albeit on a different scale. Your vision of the future should mobilize action, explain what to do and why, and invite people to join with you; however, be sure to stay aligned with the company's core message as you create this picture. For your vision, definition and clarity are more important than eloquence. Start by considering the core components of the results you want to achieve rather than how the words will flow. Once your thoughts are clear about what to do and how to do it (detailed in Chapters 5 and 6), you then can work on crafting a more vibrant story to share.

Good visions are about results, not processes. They draw in others and clearly describe the results you are seeking. Your vision needs to define something that everyone wants or can support. It needs to inspire your group to succeed, providing the guiding image of what you wish to achieve. It should be clear and specific enough that you'd know it if you had it. However, a good vision also needs to be anchored in reality—it must be attainable, and your group must be able to see and understand how it can be attained.

Three characteristics make up a good vision:

1. It should be *aspirational.* A good vision tells of what could be. It may include some ambitious goals, but it is still viewed as achievable. The goals may be hard and it may take some effort to reach them, but, ultimately, people should feel that they can bring the vision to life.
2. It should be *compelling.* The vision should be appealing and sway someone to act. The value and benefits of achieving the goals are clearly understood. The "picture of success" described by the vision is a picture of a desirable future. The vision touches emotions and gives the listener a reason for action.
3. It should be *directional.* The vision should indicate where others should go or where they will be if the vision is achieved. It defines action and a path. It is the difference between speed and velocity.

Part of the challenge in crafting a vision is making it complete and robust. What are the elements you should be thinking about? For example, when people think about retiring, they create a vision of what their life will be like—where they will live, how they will spend their days, what their expenses and income will be, who they will share time or activities with, and how their health will affect any of these elements.

Given your business setting, what are the essentials you should consider as you describe your vision? One approach is to use the categories in the Balanced Scorecard Management System, developed in the 1990s by Robert Kaplan and David Norton. As shown in Figure 3.2, the original scorecard framework measured the organization from four perspectives: Financial, Internal Business Processes, Learning and Growth, and Customer. It provided a clear prescription of what managers need to attend to in order to "balance" their efforts for the company to achieve financial success. (Kaplan and Norton, 1996)

The guiding questions included in the diagram help shape how a company thinks about its vision. This framework provides a starting point for some companies; other managers prefer to "tweak" the

FIGURE 3.2 Balanced Scorecard Example

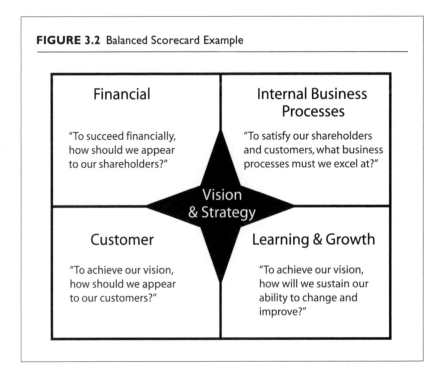

categories and questions to more aptly relate to their companies and industries. For example, an advertising agency might reframe the questions as follows:

1. *Financial.* "What kinds of services should we provide?"
2. *Internal business processes.* "To grow our clients' businesses and win more new accounts, what must we excel at?"
3. *Learning and growth.* "To achieve our vision, how will we continue to develop fresh, compelling, and breakthrough creative campaigns?"
4. *Customer.* "What kind of clients should we aim to please? What kind of image/reputation do we want to have?"

Does your organization have an existing framework that you can use to structure your vision of results and later to measure success? Your company's terminology, categories, and subcategories are likely different from the above example. Most organizations are measuring the same types of variables but tend to use industry-specific language or groupings to define the categories.

Using a variation of the balanced scorecard approach as a framework, you can describe what you hope to achieve. Remember, the goal at this stage is more about articulating clear direction than crafting an eloquent vision statement. Make sure that you have measurable factors or outcomes in your vision. These should be linked to specific goals and guidelines for measuring performance.

A balanced scorecard approach is not just used by businesses, even schools use this type of framework. Public schools are being held more accountable these days; as such, many are taking a businesslike approach to improving the product (education) that they deliver to their customers (students). Bob Eaker has worked to apply this type of thinking to schools. Coauthor of *Professional Learning Communities at Work* (Bloomington, Ind.: National Educational Service, 1998), Eaker has identified an effective strategy for helping the schools with which he works to begin to focus on results.

First, Eaker asks the school staff to develop a picture of the current conditions of the school using nothing but data. This includes defining achievement data, student behavior data, satisfaction surveys, student participation, staff activities, and the like. This hard data is then compared with the school's vision statement.

Next, he asks participants to project what the school would be like if everything in the vision is achieved in five years; in other words, what changes would be apparent in the data. When the staff begins to struggle with defining the changes, it becomes clear that the vision statement they are working from is too broad to be measurable. They then understand why results-oriented vision statements are more effective than esoteric ones. (DuFour, 2000)

DEVELOPING YOUR VISION OF RESULTS

A vision should paint the picture of success: What will success look like? It should be expressed in a way that inspires the group with attainable goals and objectives. As you create your vision of desired results, see it in the present *as if you already have it,* and put yourself

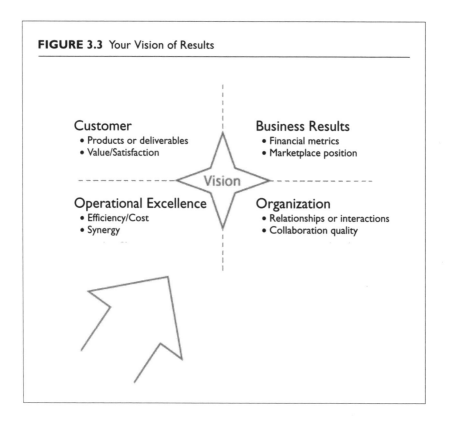

FIGURE 3.3 Your Vision of Results

and your team in the picture. Don't focus too much on the how at this point, but rather focus on the *what*—what results you want to create. Figure 3.3 zooms in on the vision component of the Breakthrough Model. Your vision should describe the results you want to achieve in each of the categories: Customers, Organization, Operational Excellence, and Business Results.

Imagine you are a syndicated cartoonist writing a daily comic strip. At present, you draw your strip and have an assistant to help you answer fan mail. Your syndicator has added you to an additional 20 newspapers this year. Your vision is to continue your daily strip and expand your output; for example, to deliver a book every other year, create a desk calendar, and have an interactive Web site with additional features about the strip and its characters.

Customers

- What products or services will you be delivering to your customers?
- How valuable will the deliverables be?
- How satisfied will your customers be?
- What type of customer relationships will you have developed?

You need to set up measures to understand whether you have achieved your vision. Your goal might be to break even after 18 months and increase your Sunday circulation by another 30 newspapers.

Business Results

- What financial results will you achieve?
- What will your position be in the marketplace?

As you bring more people on board, you will lay out ways of working that lead to the environment you want and the success you'd like. You might need to expand beyond your one room office, computer, and fax. Keeping a calendar in your head won't help the rest of the team remember holidays, deadlines, and other events. You'll have to map out the process and hand-offs for creating the comic strip, the Web site, books, and the like.

Operational Excellence

- What operating procedures will you have?
- What kind of infrastructure will be in place to support those processes?
- How will you be managing risk?
- How will operational efficiency have improved?

To meet your vision, you will need to build your close work team and expand your suppliers. You might want a collaborative team of specialists who you don't have to spend a lot of time managing. You want an open office culture, reflecting the fun and creative work that you do. The small team should feel like family—able to disagree, support each other, share opinions, and care about each other and the work they do.

Organization

- What kind of partnerships will you have?
- How will your team make decisions?
- How will people request and get help?

MOVING TO A SHARED VISION

Gaining insight into the company's strategy and using the guiding questions may have helped you develop a clearer vision of future success, but your group also will need to develop a shared vision versus a personal vision that is only meaningful to you. Robert Greenleaf, author of *Leadership Crisis,* writes: "It is the idea (vision) that unites people in the common effort, not the charisma of the leader. Optimal performance rests on the existence of a powerful shared vision that evolves through wide participation to which the key leader contributes, but which the use of authority cannot shape." (Greenleaf, 1986)

We could all probably cite examples where we've created a vision of the future to help us stay on target with our personal goals. For example, a common vision for the family holiday might be a photo of an island destination taped to a piggy bank. This plan may work— if everyone wants to go on the trip and if you think you can save enough money. However, it may be that not everyone thinks this island is the best destination, and those family members may not drop their own money into the piggy bank. A successful vision is not one that you create in isolation and then communicate to others, rather, it's a collective view that people share in and see themselves being a part of.

Vision Is Stable, but Not Static

A shared vision is not just one that everyone in the group passively agrees with, but one created using the full expertise and experience of the group. It's a vision that they all understand so well that they will instinctively know what's most important and will be able to adjust and adapt when the need arises. Given that the world we work in is fast-paced, complex, and rapidly changing, you need both the emotional and intellectual engagement of your team to meet the challenges, solve problems, and achieve results.

If each person who will play a role in achieving the vision also takes part in creating it, there is less need for later "buy-in," because it will automatically be more meaningful, desirable, and realistic for each of them. The process of creating the vision as a group helps answer the question "What does it mean for me?" for each member.

Keep in mind that a vision should be stable but not static. It needs to be regularly refreshed and updated: As new information comes in, assumptions are tested through action, and parts of the vision become real. As a manager, your role is to ensure that the relationship between planning and action stays dynamic. The following checklist will help you start the visioning process.

CHECKLIST

- ❏ Discuss your company's strategy and the parts your group will most directly support.
- ❏ Using either your company's framework or the example used here, ask each person to create a "picture" of his or her vision of the results the group will achieve in the future. A picture of results can come in different forms. Some may prefer to describe their vision in words, while others may prefer to use images. The process is less important than the results.
- ❏ Create an environment that encourages open participation. Parts of the vision may evolve through a group discussion and planning process. Other parts may leap into someone's head during the commute to work.
- ❏ People will play different roles in achieving the vision, and naturally have different perspectives of success. Provide a place to capture and reflect on all ideas. Different ideas are okay. They help people move on to more valuable dreams and visions.
- ❏ Keep it dynamic.
- ❏ After two or more discussions, agree to a vision.

WHAT'S THE CURRENT SITUATION?

Working through the Breakthrough Model, you are doing a gap analysis with an action plan. To do a gap analysis, you need to compare two elements. Creating and setting out your vision was the first element. Assessing the current situation is the second. Once you have a clear picture of both, you can understand the differences between the two and begin planning which gaps to close.

THE IMPORTANCE OF ASSESSING THE CURRENT SITUATION

Many managers put an enormous amount of effort and energy behind building and expressing their vision clearly but fail to place a similar importance on making a realistic, honest assessment of their current situation. If you move forward without making a critical and pragmatic audit of your group's starting point, you are more likely to create a plan that misjudges or even ignores some critical gaps. An off-target assessment along any of the objectives you chart has the potential to derail your future efforts. As difficult as it may be to have some of these conversations and talk honestly about the current state, you are better served having done so. Beginning with a distorted view of the tasks ahead will make your job that much more difficult.

Many times we resist taking a careful look at the present moment, especially if there are unresolved problems or issues between team members or across working groups. If you are going to work effectively as a group toward a shared vision, you have to begin with a shared view of the current situation. Be honest and forthcoming. Ignoring or misrepresenting the current state can make things seem better than they actually are, which will haunt you when you begin to implement and realize you have more work to do.

If you were to describe your current situation, what would you include? What would your team members include? Don't forget those outside your immediate group. How do you think your various stakeholders would describe the current situation? If you consider only your own or your group's perspective, you could be missing critical pieces of the whole picture. Consider how your vision will affect or need the cooperation of others around you, such as customers, partners, other departments within the organization, and external vendors, and how they view things today.

Your current situation analysis will generate both positive and negative comments. Keep in mind that where you are now is simply that—where you are now. Don't let your description of the current situation focus only on what isn't working well, but also on what *is*. Don't forget to describe the positive as well. Some aspects of how your group is working may be in a less desirable state than others. For those, focus on honestly describing the situation. Avoid assigning blame but analyze *how* you got to where you are. Consider not just what your group needs and does day to day, but also do some contingency analysis. If a crisis occurred, could your current group handle it with aplomb?

Remember that change is constant. In many cases, your current situation is simply a by-product of the complex, dynamic environment in which you work. Your "current situation" description from six months ago may have seemed OK then, but it may not match what's happening today.

There is an old piece of folklore that exists in a number of cultures and was captured in a poem by American poet John Godfrey Saxe, *The Blind Men and the Elephant*. The story goes that a number of blind men were asked to examine an elephant and describe what sort of animal they could feel with their hands. One felt the trunk of the animal; another felt the ears; another felt the bushy tail; another rubbed the ivory tusks; and another experienced the thick leathery, wrinkly skin of the animal's back leg. None of the men could "see" the whole elephant.

Each person touched a different part of the elephant and came to a different conclusion about what an elephant is like. The man touching the ears believed that an elephant is like a fan. The man touching the long and squiggly trunk thought that an elephant is like a snake, while the man touching the tail believed that an elephant is more like a rope.

A manager needs to incorporate a range of views, not just her own, as she assesses the current state. Like *The Blind Men and the Elephant*, she might think she has a tree trunk instead of an elephant's hind leg. In addition to getting multiple "close up" perspectives, a manager ought to be able to take a step back and take in the whole scene. This gives a clearer picture of reality and a wider view of the entire situation (lots of people touching an elephant and not understanding what it is they have). Linsky and Heifetz (2002) describe the ability to step back and gain perspective while remaining fiercely engaged as "getting on the balcony." In their analogy, positioning yourself on the balcony and viewing the entire "dance" gives you a much clearer view of everything that is happening (the band, the nondancers, etc.) than the perspective you have when simply a dancer on the floor.

We have made the case that you need to do an honest assessment of your current situation. We have stressed that you need to seek others' views as well. But you could gather a lot of information and still not have a well-balanced view. To make the gap analysis easier, use the same dimensions and guiding questions to describe the current state that you used to articulate your vision of the future in Chapter 3: Customers, Organization, Operational Excellence, and Business Results.

Customers

Consider what products and services you currently deliver to customers. Now consider if customers are asking for products or services you don't offer. This may be an indicator of their satisfaction and represent an opportunity for your team. The organization at large is also a customer. How valuable is your output to the company? Does it support other company products or services? As you consider the current reality, try not to just describe the current state, but think about the *why*. Why is your team where it is now vis-à-vis customers?

You can cull information to help you articulate the current situation from client satisfaction surveys, anecdotal information from group members, in-house progress reports, and other performance measures.

Consider our example of the MegaThingamajigs sales manager from Chapter 3. He has a vision to sell 50 units this year and build a solid footing to become the market leader. At present, his sales team has delivered five orders. Customers with families have been particularly responsive, while those without kids question the product's value. The manager's boss sees this product as a critical initiative and checks in regularly to understand how the sales team is doing in building the market.

Business Results

What hard data exists to measure your group's current reality? For example, are there budgets, cost-of-sales measures, customer satisfaction statistics, market share information, stock prices, or throughput rates to consider?

The MegaThingamajigs sales manager has statistics to help assess the current reality. He knows from sales reports that his sales staff has sold five products in the first quarter. He knows from the current prospect list that 15 "second calls" are set up with potential buyers. The manager knows that the sales staff currently has another 25 "hot prospects" to contact. The manager also may have some anecdotal customer satisfaction information. He may also have a specific budget allocated to the department for wooing customers during the year. For each salesperson, the manager can track individual status. This "hard data" will help the manager create the shared assessment of the current situation.

Operational Excellence

Consider how work flows through your group. Are operating procedures facilitating results or getting in the way? Do standards allow for any flexibility? What infrastructure is in place to guide workers? Are systems outdated or do they take into account changes in the industry?

Our sales manager looks at the complete process of creating and selling MegaThingamajigs. He discovers that engineering doesn't begin assembly of the product until the item is sold, which causes a delay in delivery, and negatively affects customer satisfaction. There is constant aggravation between the sales staff and the engineering department because salespeople want the product delivered ASAP. By realizing that the lag time between the sale and the delivery of the item can be solved by changing the process, the manager can improve relations between the two departments, increase customer satisfaction, and improve the reputation of the company.

Organization

How your group interacts with others will affect how you bridge the gap between current reality and vision. The organization represents the group culture, the relationships you have with others, and the quality of your collaboration. Do you have strong relationships that allow your team to serve customers and operate efficiently? Does the team itself work well together? What level of competition exists? Competition can be positive and engaging, but it also can add a layer of distraction that could hamper the process. Remember, at this point, you are simply acknowledging the situation. Consider *why* problems exist but avoid focusing on blame.

You might consider not just internal relationships but external ones as well. Some companies create close partnerships with other organizations, and so a team's results may be closely connected to how well they coordinate work with the outside groups. If you are interdependent with other groups, you should consider their "general health" as well. For example, how would changes in your suppliers' abilities affect you? Do you have any back-up resources?

The sales manager hears that his company is the one that sales-people most want to work for. At the same time, rumor has it that a well-known rival is considering introducing their own version of the MegaThingamajig. The sales team is scattered geographically and hasn't spent much time comparing experience and sharing informa-tion.

CREATING A SHARED ASSESSMENT

It's important to build a shared assessment of the current situa-tion rather than relying only on your own perspective. By including others to the extent reasonable in the process, you can build the un-derstanding, ownership, and commitment that will help make imple-menting the plans easier.

- For each dimension, state the current situation as simply as possible. The goal is not to lament the current state but to en-ergize efforts to begin moving toward the shared vision.
- Inquire as to why the current state is as it is. Don't ask who; in-stead, ask *why*. You are interested in the underlying structure and dynamics keeping things in place. Understanding this pro-vides insight into how to go about creating change efficiently.
- Assess the current situation from multiple points of view:
  - Your boss
  - Your team
  - Other internal departments
  - Customers
  - Vendors
  - Partners

BRIDGING THE GAP WITH REAL WORK
What to Do?

REVEALING THE GAPS

After building both a shared vision of the results you want to achieve and a shared assessment of the current state, you can begin to focus on the gaps between the two. Lay out the two descriptions side by side. Compare them within each category and across the whole picture. What are common threads, the stable elements to keep and improve over time? Where do the two descriptions diverge? To what degree are they different?

Figure 5.1 provides a brief example of a vision and current situation comparison along key dimensions.

The gaps and their associated challenges are what we will focus on next. Most probably will come as no surprise; you already know where some of the problem areas are. Some of your team may know as well. Now, though, you should have a clearer, more realistic picture of exactly how disparate the current state and vision are from one another, and you can begin formulating a plan to help turn that

FIGURE 5.1 Vision and Current Situation Comparison Example

Industry: Pet Supplies **Department/Team:** Online Prescription Only Products	**Company Strategy:** Be a one-stop shop for pet owners in U.S. and Canada, via mail order and Web-based catalog. We will aim for an 8% overall market share.

Vision	Current Situation
Customers: Our customers are all pet owners who require prescription pet products and prefer the convenience of ordering online. Our product selection contains the top five products in each category.	**Customers:** 15% of potential customers order prescription pet products online—primarily regular refills. Some customers think online products are inferior to what they purchase in their veterinarian's office.
Organization: Distribution agreements with drug manufacturers and veterinarians provide easy approval for customers purchasing low-risk medicines. Quick approval and delivery.	**Organization:** Some veterinarians refuse to provide approval for online refills without seeing the patient. This makes current approval process time consuming; a percentage of customers don't want to deal with the delay.
Operational Excellence: Customers have immediate access to product specialists who can answer detailed questions. Knowledge management system tracks FAQs and product updates. Web site interface becomes easier to use and more informative, reducing load on call center. Real-time inventory for supplier reordering.	**Operational Excellence:** Customers with questions about products are referred to standard catalog order team, who do not have adequate expertise. Due to long wait times, 10% of customers hang up before placing an order. Inventory is off because nonapproved orders are shown as real purchases for too long.
Business Results: Average value of customer to $600 per year. 30% of customer base ordering pet medicines. Increase market share so 5% of all pet medicines are bought from us.	**Business Results:** Average value of customer per year increased to $400. Only 14% of our catalog customers order pet medicines through our company; so 86% of customer only order other products from us.

Common Threads: catalog and Web-based business, division of larger company, continue to build on larger company's customer base, good product selection.

Gaps: Customer ease of ordering. Relationships with veterinarians and drug companies. Positioning in market. Inventory management system. Bottlenecks to information access (customers and employees). $200 average per customer; 16% more of existing customers to add pet medicines to the purchases.

group vision into reality. You need to focus yourself and your team on tangible action. The natural inclination and energy that your group has directed toward the vision is a start, but you will need more than that to sustain your energy and efforts going forward.

Once you have laid out what the gaps are, the next step is deciding which gaps to work on and how. For example, if your target results include having annual revenues equal to Y for your group, and present revenues are less than that, you'll need to consider how to grow revenue. If part of your plan entails introducing new products, do you have the people to design, manufacture, market, and distribute those new products? If not, you need to consider how you'll meet those needs—forming partnerships or alliances, finding suppliers, hiring new people, or training your current team are a few options.

Some gaps will be easier to close than others, for example, when the solution already exists and the group is ready to begin implementing it. Some gaps are extensive and you will need to create a phased plan so work is broken into more manageable segments. Some gaps will be more challenging; they may require coordinating with other groups in the organization. For some, no plan of attack may immediately present itself. Perhaps the challenge is not something you have done before or it's just not clear where to start. As a first step, it may help to lay out all of the issues and assess them in relation to one another. You might decide which ones have the potential to derail your efforts if they are not done (important/risky); which ones need to happen very soon (urgent); and which would be nice to have but are not central to reaching your vision.

You will probably find that there are many directions you can go, each one consuming time and resources. How do you decide which ones to pursue?

WORKING ON A FEW IMPORTANT THINGS

If people aren't focused on being effective and working on the right projects or tasks, they may work very hard but achieve very little. In a world of competing demands, you have to learn to focus on a few, important things. Resist the "tyranny of the urgent." Instead of reacting to every request, responding to every e-mail, and approving every project, you need to make a few strategic choices and let those choices guide everything else.

Picture a jar filled halfway with sand. If you try to fit three rocks into the jar, the rocks won't fit because the sand is taking up too much space at the bottom of the jar. Now imagine putting the rocks in another jar (the same size as the first), and then pouring the sand in. The rocks and sand will both fit! The sand fills in around the rocks; it doesn't displace them as in the first jar. The lesson: If you focus on the big stuff first, the rest will fit in around it. But if you focus too much energy on the immediate "urgent" requests (the sand), you'll be too busy to put significant effort toward strategic objectives (the big rocks). Too often the strategic objectives are what get pushed off or postponed.

In 1906, Vilfredo Pareto, an Italian economist, created a mathematical formula to describe the unequal distribution of wealth in his country—calculating that 80 percent of the wealth was owned by 20 percent of the people. Others, notably Dr. Joseph Juran, applied this formula to their own areas of expertise and observed similar phenomena. This became known as the Pareto Principle. Dr. Juran called this the principle of the "vital few and the trivial many." It also has become as adapted to the "80/20 Rule." The 80/20 Rule means that in anything, a few elements (20%) are vital and many (80%) are trivial. The value of the Pareto Principle is that it reminds you to focus 80 percent of your time on the 20 percent of tasks that matter the most. If the number of tasks or projects you could be working on seems countless and you just can't do it all, be sure to identify the vital 20 percent, and put your energy there.

If we believe that the tension between the current situation and the future vision naturally creates motivation and velocity, then you need to clearly establish the direction for your team to move along. As Figure 5.2 shows, the creative tension is weakened when your efforts are uncoordinated and heading in many different directions or when your efforts are focused on the wrong things. Don't let the number of potential challenges and projects or a lack of direction dissipate the positive energy that the group has created around the end results.

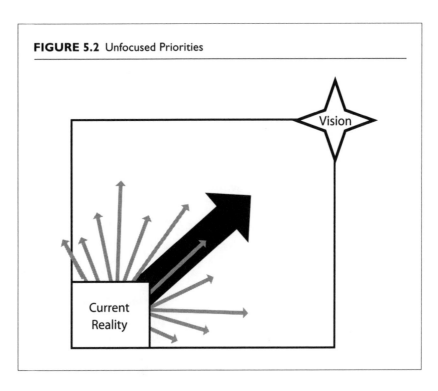

FIGURE 5.2 Unfocused Priorities

Being effective is about working on the right things, and not about just working hard. Avoid focusing too much effort on improving efficiency; instead, focus on being effective. Efficiency measures, such as better defined procedures or quicker access to accurate data, will be irrelevant unless applied to the *right* goals and objectives. Rather than taking on too many initiatives or initiatives that aren't aligned with your vision of results, *work on what is most important and where you have the most leverage.* Manage today with an eye toward the future and get clear on your priorities and initiatives.

FINDING THE MOST LEVERAGE

One way to decide what your priorities should be is to consider how well they align to the overall company strategy, where you have some discretion, and how much "bang" you will get out of pursuing one particular path compared to another.

Think of it this way: What is the value to the business and how easy or difficult will your plans be to implement? If the project isn't

Consider the newly appointed director for a manufacturing group. Her main goal for the next 18 months was to reduce the defect rate on her lines, and get her people cross-trained and up-skilled so they could take on more complex assembly jobs. She'd seen some of the preliminary designs that would be coming out of the engineering group, and knew those designs would be too difficult for her people to do right now. Unfortunately, with her appointment, she stepped in to the middle of a departmental feud between the assemblers and the quality control (QC) inspectors who worked with those lines. The assemblers thought the QC guys were whining nitpickers. The QC inspectors thought the assemblers were sloppy and defensive, and better that QC should find the assemblers' mistakes than the customers.

The director decided that getting this feud resolved was a key priority for her, and would allow her indirectly to make strides on her other goals as well. She got the two groups together and got them to agree to a common goal—to reduce defect rates by an average of 0.25 percent a month for four of the next eight months. The next step in the conversation was to discuss how to do this: What could each group do to help meet this goal? The director started by reiterating how lucky each group was to have the other, that the assemblers had people working with them who were experts in process and testing, and that the QC inspectors had technically adept and skillful partners in the assemblers.

Over time, the attitudes began to turn. QC inspectors were no longer the enemy, but were colleagues who could help turn outdated and cumbersome processes into more efficient assembly procedures. The assemblers weren't sloppy; rather, they were working under difficult conditions on products with tight tolerances. As they learned to collaborate, everyone's life got easier, the defect rate dropped, people had time to update their professional skills, and the two groups positioned themselves to take on the next generation of product . . . together.

Notice that the director didn't focus on every little thing. She defined a priority, set a clear goal, got her people to buy into it, and then rallied them around that goal. Once they had a focus—to reduce the defect rate—they made choices and decisions that aligned to it.

feasible and the results aren't valuable, you shouldn't spend the time, energy, and money doing it. If it's impossible to implement, people will get frustrated and the time, energy, and money will be wasted. The following are some questions to consider as you assess each of your possible initiatives:

Value to the Business

- What degree of potential return does it have?
- How does it contribute to your vision?
- What is the potential magnitude of the impact?
- To what degree is it aligned with current corporate strategy?
- To what degree is it aligned with your current group strategy/goals?

Ease of Implementation

- How much previous, relevant experience can you apply to this initiative or priority?
- How does the cost compare to that of other options?
- How complex is it?
- What is the risk level and probability of success?
- What degree of buy-in will you need?

In assessing your possible initiatives, it's important to remember that it's the relative difficulty that matters. There is no absolute definition for "easy" or "hard." An objective is only easy to accomplish relative to other objectives. The same applies to value to the business. "High" value is measured both according to other objectives and to the strategic goals.

Figure 5.3 offers a way to consider which projects to do. If a project is easy to complete and will have high value, it seems like a good bet to do. If a project is low value and hard to implement, it is likely one you want to avoid (the exception would be if the project outcome is a necessary precursor for a critical strategic initiative). If a project is both hard to implement *and* of high value, then consider it carefully. These projects typically are time and resource intensive, *can* be risky, and oftentimes are closely watched. On the other hand, they are often an essential step needed in order to implement the rest of the organization's strategy. A critical back-office system might fall into this category. An experimental manufacturing process might be another example. In any event, consider what the outcome

FIGURE 5.3 Priority Matrix

Value to the Business

	Easy	Medium	Hard
High	Sweet Spot	Good	Consider carefully
Medium	Good	Good	
Low			AVOID

Ease of Implementation

is you are driving for, and how well this project, initiative, people development plan, or the like, will help you realize that outcome.

You will notice that some of the blocks within the diagram in Figure 5.3 aren't given a default "value." Some decisions are not as clear-cut as the High Value + Easy to Implement = "Sweet Spot." Each challenge and situation is unique. In some cases, you may select to work on a low-value but easy project to gain some early success and traction for the group.

A FRAMEWORK FOR SEQUENCING AND STAGING

Consider the initiatives that you have selected as being the most important and generating the most leverage for the organization. You now need to think about how to sequence and stage these into objectives. What is the work to be done, when, and in what order? In this process, you will need to create manageable pieces of work and yet maintain the creative tension toward results. The vision that you have will not be achieved overnight, and, in fact, may be a target that will take several years to achieve. Intermediate milestones serve not only to break a large piece of work into more manageable pieces, but they also enable work teams to experience some early successes and maintain their forward momentum (see Figure 5.4).

We all have experience with developing capabilities over time. There are particular steps that happen before another, literally walk-

FIGURE 5.4 Focused Energies

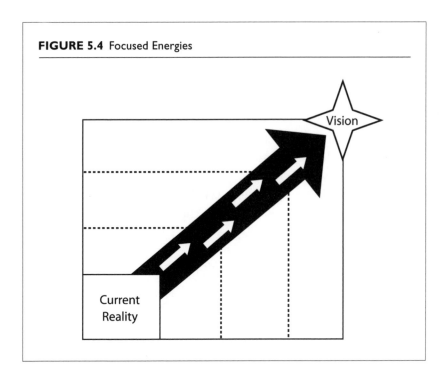

ing before running, as the saying goes. Consider some other examples of staged progression with identifiable milestones.

- *In education.* We learn and achieve particular milestones from infant to adult. The process takes many years and each milestone achieved has a little celebration, but then the child moves on to another one. For example, a child learns about numbers and counting, then simple math, such as addition and subtraction, then more complex concepts, such as fractions, long division, and algebra.
- *In business.* Someone starts a small company and grows it into a large one. He starts with a single store, a few employees, a small selection, and probably a small customer base. Products are added selectively. Staffing needs are evaluated and staff added at key growth points. Each success builds his capability to expand the business.
- *Professional athletes.* Young players may have an ultimate goal to play professionally or compete in the Olympics, but they have to go through years of developmental milestones, represent-

ing increases in skills and competitive level: Little League, high school, college, and minor leagues. Athletes progress through each level with its own milestones and successes. Each success builds on the previous success.

- *Musicians/entertainers.* They may start with beginner lessons (mastering notes, scales, and chords) and build into increasingly complex pieces and understanding of music. They may explore additional musical genres, perform in small recitals, and build skill to reach professional concerts and ensembles. They can't jump right into jazz riffs the first time they touch an instrument, but they can build their knowledge and skills to reach that point.

As a manager, you need to consider where you get the most leverage—how to achieve the results you want with an economy of means. Leverage can come from many sources. It can come from doing two things at once. It can come from planning before acting, so you get pretty close to the desired outcome the first time. It can come from taking smaller steps that make the bigger steps easier. Below are four ways to gain leverage:

I. Think Sequence

- Is there a sequence that establishes some early successes (easy/ valuable)?
- Is there a sequence that creates natural momentum (valuable/ achievable)?
- Is there an intermediate step that will help smooth the way for a bigger change?

Let's consider that your division is going to have a booth in a trade show for the first time. You've been asked to handle this project and to create the booth and ensure the show goes off well. There are a number of tasks associated with this project. For example, you'll need to get the actual booth structure and to choose what to display and how. You'll need take-away materials about the products, as well as any gift items for trade show attendees. You'll need to staff the show and to arrange the setup, takedown, and shipping for all the materials and the booth. In what order do you tackle these jobs? Are some tasks or decisions needed to be done or made before others? For example, you can't write up and design take-away materials until you've decided what to highlight.

2. Think Synergy

- Is there a sequence that builds on naturally occurring events?
- Are there others in the organization making similar changes? Can you piggyback on one another's efforts?
- Are there related initiatives with sponsorship and support that you can associate with?

As you're planning the trade show, you learn that another division is going to the same show, and a third division is doing a show three weeks before yours. Is there a way to build on their knowledge and resources? For example, you might consider a combined booth with the other division, and using the booth structure from the third. Those metal frames are expensive; there is little reason to buy a new one if you can share it with another group.

3. Think Sustainable

- Is there a sequence that builds a foundation?
- Are there infrastructure elements that, if built now, will make ongoing work easier?

This may be the first trade show your group is doing, but it may not be the last. You might consider constructing information sheets that would make the task of planning and running the booth easier the next time around.

4. Think Alignment

- What elements most support the execution of the vision?

As you select what to highlight in the show, consider where the organization is now and where you are trying to move it to. Is there a new product line to highlight or an upcoming product line that will shape the way your customers consider your company? If your strategy is to expand an existing market niche, then you might emphasize existing products, especially good sellers. Your choices should align with and support the strategy.

The goal is not simply to work harder, but to work more effectively by identifying your highest priorities and key leverage points. As a group, consider the answers to the checklist items below, making sure to seek input from everyone's experience and expertise. Remember, things are going to change, so consider your plan a work in progress and be prepared to be flexible.

CHECKLIST

- ❏ Describe the gaps between your group's current state and vision.
- ❏ Which initiatives have you identified as things that the group should be working on—the higher priority items?
- ❏ Where can you gain the most leverage?
  - Consider sequence, synergy, sustainability, and alignment.
  - Break the initiatives into smaller working pieces by developing a preliminary plan for staging milestones and objectives.

CHAPTER SIX

BUILDING ORGANIZATIONAL CAPABILITY

IN THIS CHAPTER

Manager's Role in Building Capability ■ Milestones and Needed Capabilities ■ Developing People Capability ■ Building Systems, Structure, and Processes ■ Building an Environment for Success

MANAGER'S ROLE IN BUILDING CAPABILITY

To this point, you have studied your company's strategy and the environment you're operating in. You have thought about your divisional strategy and what aspects of it your group most closely aligns with and supports. Your group has crafted a shared vision of the results you want to achieve and assessed your current state, which has led to gaining some understanding of the gaps and challenges you will face in getting to results. You have narrowed down all possible initiatives that your group *could* be focusing on to a few critical priorities, better ensuring that you are working on the right things. You have thought about the logical sequencing and staging of objectives and milestones in building the bridge to your future vision. You have a high-level plan, but now need to start moving from that high-level plan to action.

You're eager to start acting, right? You might want to wait just a minute more. It's important to think about all of the capabilities that you will need to actually achieve the results that you want. Consider what unique combination of skills and resources you will need to reach each of your priority goals. As a manager, your role is to anticipate, identify, and build capabilities for the future. It is too late to think about the capabilities once the need is here.

"Did you think the ladder of success would be straight up?"

MILESTONES AND NEEDED CAPABILITIES

"Most organizations are well-prepared for problems that no longer exist."
John Croft

For each of your larger key initiatives, you now should have some identified milestones or intermediate steps, along with a plan for sequence and staging. We consider each stage's capability needs individually, because the capabilities that you need for a later milestone will not be the same ones that you need today. At the same time, consider if there are synergies between what you will need for one stage and what you will need for another.

The Changing Roles of Librarians

James H. Billington is the Librarian of Congress. He is in charge of the "largest library in the world, with nearly 128 million items on approximately 530 miles of bookshelves. The collections include more than 29 million books and other printed materials, 2.7 million recordings, 12 million photographs, 4.8 million maps, and 57 million manuscripts . . ." (Library of Congress 2004) He is leading the Library through what he describes as. . . . the greatest upheaval in the transmission of knowledge since the invention of the printing press . . ." (Library of Congress, Strategic Plan), and has to ensure that the Library can meet the needs of a multimedia and increasingly digitized world. Dewey Decimal systems and card catalogs are being replaced by online databases with search functions.

One of the projects the library has is the National Digital Information Infrastructure and Preservation Program. Its aim is to create an architecture to preserve digital content and build a network of partners to provide archiving and access services into the future. This program represents a shift because librarians primarily used to help someone find a book or microfiche. It was a matter of locating and interpreting relevant information. Some specialists had expertise in preserving or repairing old documents. For this project, however, librarians are being asked to head a project to design how to collect and store information—to create the *idea* of a book or microfiche instead of just locating it.

If you were leading this project, where would you start? The first question is: "What do we need to be capable of to execute our strategy and achieve our goals?" In this case, the new capability is a digital information infrastructure. The second, "What unique combination of work processes, systems, structure, people, and work environment would we need to have in place to transform our traditional library into this new digital information age?"

As was noted previously, you can't work on everything at once. In thinking about building capabilities, you will essentially follow the same approach used to determine key initiatives—assess what capabilities you need to accomplish your objectives, assess what capabilities you have today, and then plan how to build and bridge the gap.

Begin with a *description of the intermediate step or objective.*

Rather than relying on a single-line bullet point that is open to varied interpretation, describe *in detail* exactly what it is you want to achieve. Just as with your future vision or current situation assessment, everyone needs to be in sync and clear on what is expected for each milestone. This includes both the people who will be working on the project and those who are interested in seeing or using the end results in some way.

This is especially important for large-scale projects that involve many steps. Those who are most interested in the final product tend to focus on the end results and not the many interim objectives along the way. Be clear what the objective is at each stage so that people are not expecting one thing and you are delivering something else. If your milestone objective is to deliver a first effort—such as an initial design, a first draft of a manuscript, or a mockup prototype of a customer Web site—describe what that means so that everyone is clear. For example, if you think that you are creating a visual representation of how a client Web site might look and feel but the customer thinks you are delivering a first release with real moving parts, you may have a problem.

Identifying the right priorities and key points of leverage is a start, but achieving your objectives requires more. For each of the objectives or milestones that you've identified, what will it take to actually deliver the desired results? As Figure 6.1 indicates, for each of your objectives, there are critical deliverables, progress measures, and capabilities—people, processes, or environment—that are needed to support your efforts.

As you consider your group, ask yourself: What do I owe to my boss or customers? What are my *deliverables* or *outputs?* What value do they add? When are they due? Be specific about what you owe to each of your various stakeholder groups, including your boss, other divisions or departments, and your customers. It may not be the same for each group. One stakeholder may need the technical specifications of a product while another needs the graphical design requirements.

FIGURE 6.1 Staging Milestones and Capabilities

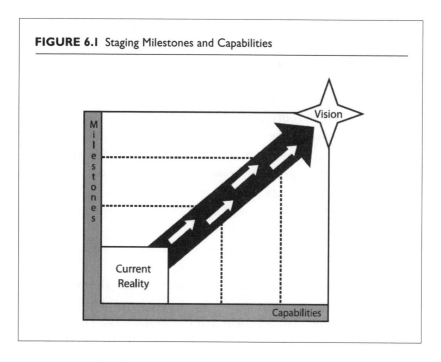

What *metrics* or *measures* of progress and success will you use? What is your target budget? What is your delivery time line? Is there a firm, agreed on completion date? Is everyone aware of the time line?

What particular blend or mix of *capabilities* are needed to accomplish the objective? Capabilities span a range of elements.

- *People.* What skills, expertise, certifications, attitudes, energy, or time is needed, available, or missing? For example, a project may require someone who has expertise with a particular software program or someone with an eye for detail.
- *Systems and processes.* What operating procedures, standards, work methods, or infrastructure are in place, in the way, or missing? What technologies would extend your capabilities? What do you need to build for the future? For example, a specialty retailer located in a small town experienced a dip in sales when a large company shut down its local operation. Instead of shutting its doors, the shop decided to expand its nascent mail-order business. This required a new way of doing sales that included creating a Web presence and an updating schedule, adopting an

online ordering system, contracting differently with a shipping company, and shifting its modest advertising strategy. As the business was changing, the shop staff needed to change their way of working as well.

- *Work environment.* What kind of work environment supports the vision? What group culture, feeling, relationships between people, or partnerships are needed, available, or missing? For example, start-up firms are often short of money and the people who work there put in long hours, doing the job of two or three people. The intensity of creating a new organization bonds people together and creates a strong feeling of ownership. However, the hours and range of tasks people perform in a start-up might not be accepted by people who work in a large, mature firm.

- *Structure.* How is your group organized to do the work? Your structure should be driven by the strategy, and able to support, enhance, and drive the plan that you have designed. Will some groups work more closely in the future? Is there an existing hierarchy that will hinder your efforts? You should also consider the structure that will be needed in the future when much of your vision and objectives will have been accomplished.

Rather than just thinking through the answers to these questions or discussing them verbally, it is a good idea to go through the steps of recording the details of your objectives. Actually writing down a description of your objectives, deliverables, due dates, and required capabilities can force a level of clarity that might be missing otherwise. And everyone needs to be clear on what the goals and requirements are. Figure 6.2, the Sample Intermediate Step Definition Chart at the end of this chapter, provides an example of how to approach defining an objective.

Once you have completed a general assessment of the capabilities needed for each of your milestones or objectives, it's time to *think about the gaps* that exist in each area and what options there are for filling those gaps. In some cases, you might revamp and reuse what exists today. In other cases, you may need to build from the ground up. To do that, you have to accurately assess your current capabilities.

One line manager described a situation where her company had received a contract to manufacture and deliver a very specialized piece of medical equipment. There would be more frequent quality checks and less room for error—a slightly new environment for the existing workers. The customer would be more involved in the process and more visible on location. Because of the shortened production schedule, the processes and workflow would have to be more stringently documented and followed. In addition, there would be some alterations to the equipment used in the process, and, therefore, workers would have to be trained in a slightly new method.

When assessing what capabilities would be needed for the new project, she knew that she would need people who were very attentive to detail and product specifications, but who could also work quickly to keep the project on schedule. The project manager would have to have strong organization skills to create and manage the more complex processes. The entire team would have to become accustomed to interacting more frequently with the client team and adapting to their needs.

DEVELOPING PEOPLE CAPABILITY

Your ability to achieve results depends on having the right people, in the right roles, with the right skills, working on the tasks that are most important. Remember the 80/20 rule: 80 percent of the effort should be spent on 20 percent of the issues. Managers have an obligation to help attract, develop, and retain talent to meet the organization's needs. They also must assess, coach, and develop their existing people, both to address individual aspirations and to meet the future needs of the organization. Some of that development is general, such as helping them to develop broader skill sets, including managing meetings or defining goals clearly using SMART goals: Specific, Measurable, Achievable, Relevant, and Timely. Some of it is unit specific, such as using proprietary software or operating a piece of equipment.

The first step in developing people capability is figuring out what the core competencies are that will enable you to meet the key objectives and initiatives that you have outlined. What are the few, critical skills or areas of expertise that will make the difference between success and failure?

You can use the Sample People Capability Assessment Chart in Figure 6.3 for the next step, which is to assess what exists today—the current state. What are your team members' strengths, challenges, aspirations, and areas for development? This is not a performance evaluation, but simply a capabilities assessment to guide future development—both for their needs and yours. There are usually multiple options for addressing capability needs, including building, buying, and borrowing, but you first need to understand the current state to judge which of these methods will offer the best way to close the gap.

What are your team members' key *strengths or challenges?* In what areas do they excel? Where do they struggle? Why? This should include a wide range of capabilities, especially any competencies identified as critical by the organization. Examples include people skills, technical skills, presentation skills, project management, problem solving, functional expertise (such as accounting or marketing), industry expertise (own industry or that of clients), basic managerial experience, coaching and development of others, or simply historical knowledge of the company.

What are their *aspirations* for career development? Are they new at their current role and want to remain there for some time? Do they want to acquire additional technical training or certifications for their current role? Are there different roles within the company that they would like to develop into eventually? What are their priorities for their time—family, community, work, pastimes?

Based on their strengths, challenges, and aspirations, and on the firm's future needs, what *growth opportunities* can you provide them? Most people learn best when learning in context, that is, on the job. Given your teams' current skills and experience, what *areas for development* exist based on the key initiatives you'd like to implement? How can the needs be addressed? Which gaps will be the highest priorities to fill in the coming year?

A **professional services** firm was growing its business. As the office manager looked at the next year's needs, he decided he needed two more people to lead customer teams. He picked two people who were rising stars; they were smart and could learn how to run their own team in short order. He thought they would be perfect. What he forgot to consider was how they saw their career paths, what they wanted to do. As he spoke to one, the office manager learned that the person he wanted to promote had no interest in leading a team, but rather wanted to stay as a supporting player and grow in that role. At that point, the office manager turned to the outside and hired a new team leader from another firm. The second (internal) person was thrilled to be promoted. The office manager consulted with her and they determined what skills she needed to build in the next year and how, as well as what level of work her team should take on. By year's end, the new hire was doing wonderfully and the promoted person was gaining skills and confidence; she could ably fill her new role.

BUILDING SYSTEMS, STRUCTURE, AND PROCESSES

What are systems? You may immediately think of large scale, online systems implemented across the organization, such as accounting or human resources systems. Certainly, those are critical resources, but systems are also the interconnected routines, structures, procedures, and processes that you use each day. They can be both formal and well documented, and informal and "understood."

Why do we have systems? In many cases, they have been created as a result of particular situations—such as what to do when something occurs that is out of the normal pattern—so that people know how to respond in the future. As the size and complexity of our work increases, systems can help coordinate and control how we work. We maximize our performance by developing procedures and processes to streamline and simplify our efforts. Hopefully, this results in cost savings and economies of scale, efficient processes and standard operating procedures, and divisions of labor that make the most of our experts.

Like all other aspects of the organization today, systems have to be evaluated and adjusted on a regular basis to keep in step with future needs. This could mean anything from a slight adjustment, to significant reworking, to a complete overhaul. To achieve the results that you envision, you will need to assess the capability of existing systems to meet your future needs. How do they support your current efforts and what changes need to be made to build solutions for the future? How will changes to one system affect other systems? Or other groups within the organization? Like a spider's web, if you pull a string on one edge, the effects are felt throughout. None of the silk strands making up the web is independent, but rather acts together with the other strands. As a manager in the center of the organization, you are in the best position to understand the interdependencies and influence change.

For each of your key initiatives, consider what systems (procedures, policies, and standards) will be needed to support your efforts. What is in place today and what will you need in the future? The table in Figure 6.4 lists typical systems within an organization. Create your own list and evaluate how each may support or hinder progress with each initiative.

Given your assessment of how current systems support or hinder your efforts, what capabilities are needed for the future? If a system isn't optimal, that is, it hinders your efforts or is ineffective, what will you do to improve its capabilities? Often, our first line of action is to make changes in the margins, or work around the problem. This may be effective in the short term, but doesn't build sustainable capability for the organization. Often, workarounds unknowingly cause new problems elsewhere.

You may have to advocate for wholesale changes to current systems rather than solving problems with minor adjustments. Again, you can't do everything. Consider what systems adjustments or additions will be most critical to your initiatives, and when they will need to be in place. What are your options for influencing change around each system? How long will it take? What are the implications and effects of change?

In addition to systems that can aid your efforts, consider what associated *technologies* can help or hinder your particular efforts:

- Accurate data
- Quick access
- Virtual meetings
- Digital imaging
- Enhanced security
- Voice over Internet Protocol (VoIP)
- Newly developed equipment
- Web research tools
- Global Positioning Systems (GPS)
- Telecommunications
- Advanced manufacturing technologies
- Business simulations

Whatever your industry focus, it's likely that some technologies can provide a competitive advantage when applied strategically. What technologies will better enable your group to achieve their desired results? Are you looking ahead and evaluating emerging technologies and their potential benefits to the company and your initiatives? As with existing systems, opportunities to apply technologies need to be evaluated on an ongoing basis. Figure 6.4, the Sample Systems and Technologies Capability Assessment Chart at the end of this chapter, provides an example of how to approach analyzing your systems and technology current capabilities and future needs.

BUILDING AN ENVIRONMENT FOR SUCCESS

Translating strategy into behavior does not always easily follow according to plan. Even when people agree in principle with a new strategic direction, it will take time for them to actually behave differently. Old habits die hard, as the saying goes. As a manager, what can you do to create and reinforce an environment and culture that is consistent with the strategic direction and the long-term results you are trying to achieve?

To start, be cognizant of your own preferences and behaviors and ways in which you need to adapt as well. Your own decisions and approaches to doing business day-to-day should be consistent with the rest of your plan, including your vision, priorities, milestones, and plans for building capability. Be consistent between what you say and what you do. If you want your people to act as a team, then don't demand only individual-level outputs. Make sure there are shared goals and shared responsibilities.

What aspects of the culture and environment will have the most impact on your efforts?

- *Coaching and mentoring.* How are people coached when working through new tasks? Are mistakes used as learning opportunities? Do people have opportunities to interact with and learn from the more seasoned staff? Are people provided opportunities to gain additional technical training and certification?
- *Innovative approaches to problem solving.* Are a variety of people included in brainstorming and problem-solving sessions? Does the work environment support borrowing resources and cross-functional teams? Are there resources dedicated to research and development? Are first prototypes allowed to fail?
- *Seeking and developing partnerships.* Where is it most efficient to build your own capabilities and where does it make more sense to create partnerships and alliances? Are you actively seeking external partnerships?

FIGURE 6.2 Sample Intermediate Step Definition Chart

Intermediate step or objective. Describe in detail exactly what you want to achieve with this objective.

Deliverables. Describe what outputs you will deliver to particular stake-holders—your boss, other teams, customers, and the like. The deliverable may not be the same for each group.

Measures of progress and success. Define how you will measure success and completion. Include target budget, delivery time line, and completion date.

Capabilities Needed to Accomplish

People. Describe the skills, expertise, certifications, attitudes, energy, or time that is needed for this objective.

Systems and processes. Describe the operating technologies, procedures, standards, work methods, or infrastructures that are needed for this objective.

Work environment. Describe the work culture—relationships between people, collaboration, innovation, competition, partnerships—that is needed for this objective.

Structure. Consider how your current structure will either support or hinder your efforts to achieve this objective. What changes will you need to make?

FIGURE 6.3 Sample People Capability Assessment Chart

Consider the future roles and capabilities that your team will need to fill to be successful in achieving the results you want. With these in mind, complete an analysis of each team member's current capabilities (strengths and challenges) and future aspirations. What growth opportunities and areas for development does this provide for them?

Team Member

Strengths. In what areas does he or she excel? Why?

Challenges. In what areas does he or she struggle? Why?

Aspirations. Where would he or she like to be in the future?

Growth opportunities/Areas for development.

FIGURE 6.4 Sample Systems and Technologies Capability Assessment Chart

Milestone or Objective. Describe your milestone or objective.

The table below lists typical systems and technologies within an organization. Replace these examples with ones that are applicable to your objectives. Describe how each, in its current state, supports or hinders your efforts. Outline possible approaches for influencing, changing, or developing the system or technology capability that you need. Keep in mind how changes in one area might affect other systems or other users.

Systems	*Staffing*	*Performance Management*	*Procurement*	*Business Planning*	*Other*
Supports					
Hinders					
Influence or Change					
Technologies	*Digital Imaging*	*Voice over IP*	*GPS*	*Web Conferencing*	*Other*
Supports					
Hinders					
Influence or Change					

CHAPTER SEVEN

MAKING IT HAPPEN

Directing People's Attention ■ Measuring the Right
Things ■ Being a Role Model ■ The Process Continues

At this point, you have created a plan to align your group's work
with your overall company strategy. You first gathered information
to understand the strategy. Then you began the translation process,
considering how your group best supports aspects of the overall
strategy. You have prioritized objectives based on your strategy, value
to the business, and ease of implementation. You did a gap analysis
to understand what changes you might need to begin making so that
your team is better positioned to implement the future stages of the
strategy. You also did an inventory of other resource needs, planning
the capabilities that will need to be developed for the future. Finally,
you are at the stage to bring your plans to life. You now need to make
it happen.

How do you make it happen? How do you focus people on the
right tasks and projects? How do you ensure both performance today
and development to meet future needs? What will give you the most
leverage as a leader?

DIRECTING PEOPLE'S ATTENTION

There are several methods that leaders can use to focus people's attention. A primary and quite explicit way is in the goal-setting process. Managers can help their people set goals that align well with the team's goals and can help with developing skills needed in the near future.

Another way is through the management routines they set up. If a manager has a weekly meeting, and every week she asks her direct reports the same set of five questions, then the direct reports will quickly realize what they need to pay attention to in the coming week. They will know that they will need the answers each week, and are more likely to notice events relating to those topics.

A third method is coaching and offering feedback. This works two ways: first, in what the manager chooses to give feedback on, and second, in the way it's done. Coaching is an opportunity to share experience and best practices, and support someone as he or she tries a new skill. Consider the naturally occurring events that allow you to reinforce or redirect someone, for example, through answering an e-mail or voice mail.

MEASURING THE RIGHT THINGS

Think carefully about what you measure. People respond to what they think others are watching and valuing. There is a classic business article by Steven Kerr (1975) titled "On the Folly of Rewarding A while Hoping for B." It details many situations where followers didn't act the way leaders wanted. "It's the reward system, stupid." For example, the author notes that in academics, good research is often highly rewarded while good teaching is not. In sports, although team effort is what we say we value, the ballplayer that leads in assists or hits the most sacrifice flies is not as highly recruited or rewarded as the player who makes the goals or scores the runs. Kerr's main point is that we can't expect people to do the things we say they should do when we are rewarding something else.

As a manager, you can help people focus by setting specific and thoughtful measures and rewards. So, if you care about it, measure it. If you don't care about it, don't measure it. Having a clear standard makes it obvious if they did or did not meet the expectations. Just like the academic example above, if you care about teaching and mentoring, don't just reward people based on the amount of their published research. If you value innovation and risk taking, recognize that failure goes hand-in-hand and don't just reward error-free results.

You must be aware that some tasks, such as scoring baskets, tend to be highly visible while others, such as calling the defensive plays or providing leadership on the field, are not. In a business setting, team building and creativity may not get rewarded simply because they are harder to observe. That, however, shouldn't excuse you from recognizing those who are creative or those who help keep the team together.

BEING A ROLE MODEL

Finally, you are a leader. As such, you are a role model for others in the organization. Show them how to act, demonstrate what your priorities are, and enact the culture you want to create.

If learning is important, demonstrate that you also are working on self-improvement and strengthening your abilities. Get "caught" with a professional journal. Enroll in self-study, management, or technical classes, or professional seminars. Use self-assessments, such as a 360° Leadership evaluation or self-assessment instruments (e.g., Myers-Briggs Type Indicator or Emotional Intelligence—EQ), to provide insights into your personal preferences, values, and behaviors.

Handle crises in a way that clarifies what is and what isn't important. When things go wrong, assume responsibility rather than looking for others to blame. Assess the situation, make adjustments, coach others on how to improve in the future, and move on.

Finally, tell stories. Convince others to tell their stories. People tell stories as a way to make sense of the world around us, as a way to infuse structure and meaning in our daily lives, and as a way to connect our life experiences to others. We use stories to teach (e.g., Aesop's Fables) and to get people to act (e.g., Martin Luther King, Jr.'s, or Mahatma Gandhi's speeches). People will be more likely to remember the message and to connect to it with both their heads and their hearts.

THE PROCESS CONTINUES

Completing an initial version of your action plan doesn't mean that you can stop planning. We've used the Breakthrough Model to help you visualize the pieces and steps toward attaining your strategic vision, but walking through the model can make it seem as though it is a linear process, with a clean, direct path from current reality to future vision. If only it were that simple. Reaching your future vision is accomplished more through a series of small gains—of deliverables and milestones and capabilities—and you are only at the first stage. Many of these initial priorities will be the building blocks that form the foundation for future goals. At each step, reassess where you are, where you are going, and the capabilities you need to move on to the next level.

This is a building process, and a process through which you will continue to make choices and adjustments. Return to the guiding principles we began with in Chapter 1 to help you stay aligned.

- *Continue to be a student.* The environment and competition is continually changing. Don't fall behind.
- *Continue to create meaning.* Connect others to the new things that you learn as a student and keep adding to the strategy story.
- *Continue to be honest.* Reassess capabilities, current situation, and progress. Make honest adjustments and move on.

- *Continue to think capabilities.* Capabilities provide you competitive advantage and enable you to reach milestones. And actively building people capability engages individuals in the strategy.
- *Continue to get comfortable with change.* The world is dynamic and your firm's strategy *will* be as well. Be proactive and embrace change. It keeps things interesting.

BIBLIOGRAPHY

BB&T. 2004. http://www.bbandt.com/about/. Accessed December 2004.

Bossidy, Larry, and Ram Charan. 2002. *Execution: The Discipline of Getting Things Done.* New York: Crown Business.

Croft, John. 1970. *Journal of Applied Behavioral Science* 6, no. 1.

Davidson, John, with John Steinbreder. 2000. *Hockey for Dummies.* New York: Hungry Minds, Inc.

DuFour, Rick. 2000. "Community: Data Put a Face on Shared Vision." *Journal of Staff Development* 21, no. 1 (Winter, http://www.nsdc .org/library/publications/jsd/dufour211.cfm).

Fritz, Robert. 1991. *Creating.* New York: Ballantine Books.

———. 1999. *The Path of Least Resistance for Managers.* San Francisco: Berrett-Koehler Publishers.

George, Nicholas, and Adam Jones. 2004. "Absolut Is Feeling the Chill in a Changing Global Vodka Market." *Financial Times.* 18 November: 14.

Greenleaf, Robert K. 1986. *The Leadership Crisis: A Message for College and University Faculty.* Newton Center, MA: Robert K. Greenleaf Center.

Hambrick, Don, and J. W. Fredrickson. 2001. "Are You Sure You Have a Strategy?" *Academy of Management Executive* (15, no. 4: 48–59).

Hamel, Gary, and C. K. Prahalad. 1994. *Competing for the Future.* Boston: Harvard Business School Press.

Hammonds, Keith. 2001. "Porter's Big Ideas," *Fast Company,* 44:150 (March).

Heinz, H. J. 2003. *H. J. Heinz Annual Report.* (http://www.heinz.com/ 2003annualreport/splash.html) Accessed December, 2004.

Hewitt, Gordon and C.K. Prahalad. 2005. *Creating Corporate Value in the New Competitive Landscape.* Unpublished.

Kaplan, Robert S., and David P. Norton. 1996. *The Balanced Scorecard: Translating Strategy into Action.* Boston: Harvard Business School Press.

Kerr, Steven. 1975. "On the Folly of Rewarding A While Hoping for B." *Academy of Management Journal* 18: 769–83.

Kotter, John P. 1996. *Leading Change.* Boston: Harvard Business School Press.

The Library of Congress. 2004. *About the Library.* http://www.loc.gov/about/. Accessed December, 2004.

The Library of Congress. http://www.loc.gov/about/history/pdfs/04-08StrategicPlan2-3.pdf. "Letter from the Librarian." *Strategic Plan Fiscal Years 2004–2008:* 2–3.

Linsky, Marty, and Ronald A. Heifetz. 2002. *Leadership on the Line: Staying Alive through the Dangers of Leading,* Boston, MA: Harvard Business School Press.

Nohria, Nitin, William Joyce, and Bruce Roberson. 2003. "What Really Works." *Harvard Business Review* (July).

Orlick, Terry. 2000. *In Pursuit of Excellence.* Human Kinetics Publishers.

Porter, Michael E. 1980. *Competitive Strategy: Techniques for Analyzing Industries and Competitors.* New York: The Free Press.

Ranbaxy Laboratories Limited. 2003. *Annual Report.* http://www.ranbaxy.com/ar2003/images/ar2003.pdf. Accessed November 2004.

Rand, Ben. 2004. "Kodak Overhauling Culture in an Effort to Refocus Product Development." *Democrat and Chronicle* National Metro: 1A, 10A. (21 November).

Royal Dutch Petroleum. 2003. *Annual Report.* http://www.shell.com/html/investor/en/reports2003/rd/c/c6.html. Accessed December 2004.

Senge, Peter M., et al. 1994. *The Fifth Discipline Fieldbook.* New York: Doubleday.

Ulrich, Dave and Norm Smallwood. 2003. *Why the Bottom Line Isn't: How to Build Value through People and Organization.* Hoboken, NJ: John Wiley & Sons, Inc.

Wells, Stuart. 1998. *Choosing the Future.* Butterworth-Heinemann.

Wilhelm, Warren R. 2003. *Learning Architectures: Building Organizational & Individual Learning.* GCA Press.

INDEX

Share the message!

Bulk discounts
Discounts start at only 10 copies and range from 30% to 55% off retail price based on quantity.

Custom publishing
Private label a cover with your organization's name and logo. Or, tailor information to your needs with a custom pamphlet that highlights specific chapters.

Ancillaries
Workshop outlines, videos, and other products are available on select titles.

Dynamic speakers
Engaging authors are available to share their expertise and insight at your event.

Call Dearborn Trade Special Sales at 1-800-621-9621, ext. 4444,
or e-mail trade@dearborn.com.

Dearborn™
Trade Publishing
A **Kaplan Professional** Company